The Punch Book of
UTTERLY BRITISH HUMOUR

Also published by Grafton Books

The Punch Book of Cricket
The Punch Book of Golf
The Punch Book of Health
The Punch Book of Sex and Marriage
Travelling Light – Punch Goes Abroad
Fun Fare: The Punch Book of Food and Drink

THE PUNCH BOOK OF
UTTERLY BRITISH HUMOUR

Edited by
Amanda-Jane Doran

Introduction by
David Thomas

GRAFTON BOOKS

A Division of the Collins Publishing Group

LONDON GLASGOW
TORONTO SYDNEY AUCKLAND

Grafton Books
A Division of the Collins Publishing Group
8 Grafton Street, London W1X 3LA

Published by Grafton Books 1989
Reprinted in paperback (twice) 1990

Copyright © Punch Publications Limited 1989

British Library Cataloguing in Publication Data

The Punch book of utterly British humour
1. Humour in English. 1900—Anthologies
I. Doran, Amanda-Jane   II. Punch
827'.912'08

ISBN 0–246–13502–6
ISBN 0–246–13741–X (Pbk)

Printed and bound in Great Britain by
Butler & Tanner Ltd, Frome and London

All rights reserved. No part of this publication may be
reproduced, stored in a retrieval system, or transmitted,
in any form, or by any means, electronic, mechanical,
photocopying, recording or otherwise, without the prior
permission of the publisher.

CONTENTS

LIST OF CONTRIBUTORS

WRITERS

Kenneth Allsop 66
Alex Atkinson 121, 152
John Betjeman 115
Basil Boothroyd 50, 95
Melvyn Bragg 166
Caryl Brahms 29
Alan Brien 13
Tina Brown 26
Michael Bywater 126, 139
Hugh Chesterman 85
John Cleese 20
Alan Coren 76, 105
Mary Dunn 23
Richard Gordon 17, 156
George Grossmith 39
David Hunt 129
Frank Keating 64
Brigid Keenan 122
Miles Kington 53, 91
Percival Leigh 37

Ann Leslie 169
Humphrey Lyttelton 133
Lord Mancroft 100
Fay Maschler 137
George Melly 147
Michael Parkinson 61
Libby Purves 41, 58
Stanley Reynolds 69
Jonathan Sale 173
W. C. Sellar 86
Ned Sherrin 29
G. W. Stonier 160
David Taylor 33, 47
William Makepeace Thackeray 72
David Thomas 7
Auberon Waugh 83
Geoffrey Willans 113
Angus Wilson 143
P. G. Wodehouse 103
R. J. Yeatman 86

CARTOONISTS

Albert 147
Anton 22, 45, 49
Ardizzone 161
Banx 123, 155
Bateman 28
Lewis Baumer 29
Baxter 89
George Belcher 12, 159
Hector Breeze 95, 112, 117
Eric Burgin 143
Chic 132
Diz 161
Donegan 51, 136, 153
Richard Doyle 38
George Du Maurier 17, 41
Duncan 134, 135, 157
Emett 119
ffolkes 32, 90, 98, 120, 139
Ed Fisher 39
Noel Ford 87
Fougasse 36
Bud Grace 57
Graham 168
David Haldane 105
Merrily Harpur 79
Heath 124, 132
Hoffnung 112
Tony Holland 27
Holte 42, 46, 175
Martin Honeysett 82, 96, 149
Vernon Kirby 152

David Langdon 16, 71, 130
Larry 56, 111
John Leech 65, 75, 167
Lowry 46, 162
Ed McLachlan 109, 165
Stan McMurtry 164
Marc 94
David Myers 156
Nick Newman 82
Pont 21, 50, 63, 80, 103, 116, 125, 131, 140, 173
Ken Pyne 15
Raven Hill 136
E. T. Reed 85
Scully 114
Ronald Searle 11, 118
Sillince 128
E. H. Shepard 72, 117
Siggs 117
Smilby 138
Sprod 35, 102, 115, 145, 154
J. W. Taylor 44, 52, 163
William Makepeace Thackeray 73, 74
Thelwell 59, 150–151, 163
Thorpe 60
Bill Tidy 170–171
Wallis Mills 142, 146
Arthur Watts 110
Mike Williams 19, 81, 99, 107, 148
Mervyn Wilson 25
Kevin Woodcock 158

INTRODUCTION

by David Thomas

Goodness knows why they'd want me to introduce this book. Asking the Editor of *Punch* to introduce a book about British humour is like asking the England team manager to preface a work on British football. Both jobs are filled by men who are supposed to know what they are doing. But everyone knows that they're hopeless. *Punch* isn't funny. England always lose. It's common knowledge.

The only consolation, as I open my morning postbag, or as Mr Bobby Robson opens his morning papers – I'm assuming, rashly, that *The Sun* won't have had him fired by the time you read these words – is that it's always been like that. England have been losing to continental no-hopers for as long as anyone can remember. As for *Punch* . . . a century ago a reader complained to Francis Burnand, the magazine's fourth Editor, that *Punch* was not as funny as it used to be. Dryly, he replied, 'It never was.'

In fact, it's a racing certainty that Mark Lemon, the founding Mr Punch, received a sackful of letters in 1841 soon after the publication of his second edition and that they all told him that it wasn't as funny as the first. The problem is that, just as every football fan is certain that they know the best team for England, so every *Punch* reader – not to mention a million others who never look at the magazine – is certain that he or she has the magical formula required to make it funny.

People are very touchy about their sense of humour. It's no good saying to them, 'Well, the reason you didn't laugh is not because the article wasn't funny. It's because you're a sourfaced old bat who wouldn't get a joke if it was spelled out for you in neon letters ten feet high.' If you say things like that, they're apt to get offended. It would be like criticising their driving, or their cooking, or their abilities in bed.

Not that this – as any comic will tell you – prevents vicious complaints from audiences who came in search of laughter and failed to get it. Do romantic novelists get hate mail if they fail to induce tears by the end of Chapter Five? Is the Editor of the *Independent* magazine deluged with disapproval if his product fails to induce deep sleep? I can't be certain, but I doubt it.

It's enough to make you wonder why anyone would ever want to be funny. For one thing, it's incredibly difficult. P. G. Wodehouse, for example, might appear to float along in a delightful cloud of effortless innocence, but you try doing it.

Bertie Wooster's idle jollity is the product of brilliant talent allied to years of practice. If Wodehouse had wanted an easy life he could have cut out all the jokes, flung in lots of long words, added a dash of pretension, flambéed three light statements of the obvious, baked the lot in four hundred pages of the utmost tedium and – hey presto! – they'd have been queueing up to give him prizes. That he forswore the siren song of seriousness in favour of the rocky road that leads to Market Blandings is an act of self-sacrifice for which we should all be eternally grateful.

Wodehouse wrote for *Punch* for sixty years, on and off, between 1902 and 1962. For fifty-three of those years he lived in the USA, yet his work is still regarded as the epitome of that celebrated institution, the British Sense of Humour. The BSH is a bit like the British Gentleman, or the British Teatime, one of those nebulous ideas which go to make up the notion of what Britain is in the eyes of the outside world.

There are those who pooh-pooh our jokes and our chaps and our teas because they aren't sufficiently relevant or multi-cultural or progressive for the World of Today. I, however, would rather pooh-pooh the idea of 'relevance' – *so* 1968, don't you think? – and just feel grateful every time the world thinks of our sense of humour when it could be thinking of our hooligans. But that still begs a question, viz. what is it, this great British Sense of Humour? What does it look like? How will the man-or-woman-in-the-street recognise it? How does it differ from, say, the Bulgarian Sense of Humour? And have we geared up for the coming of Euro-laughter in 1992?

Questions like that are Very British. It's the old Escalating Absurdity gag. That's the one where you start with something pretty reasonable, then stretch the concept up to and beyond the point where it becomes silly. Add a splash of surrealism and an Oxbridge education and you've got that loony lineage that stretches from the Goons, through Prince Charles, to Monty Python and beyond.

Mind you, those questions weren't any odder than the ones I was asked by a gentleman from *Pravda* recently. He had a list of fifteen queries ranging from, 'What is your favourite TV show?' to 'What is the responsibility of humour in the age of *perestroika*?' His desire to speak to Mr Punch may have been an example of *glasnost*, but I suspect it was actually part of the KGB's top secret Sense of Humour project, designed to teach their spies the right jokes so that they can blend unobtrusively into British conversations.

There's another Famous British Joke, in this case Making Fun of Foreigners, in which you take the mickey out of anyone who speaks with a different accent. Of course, we don't have to go abroad to do this (thanks to that classic British gag, the Class System), which is one of the reasons why the only joke more popular than Making Fun of Foreigners is making Fun of Ourselves.

Self-mockery is a crucial aspect of the world's funniest societies. Jewish humour is based upon it, as is Polish. In those two cases the mockery is a matter of self-defence, Poles and Jews being two of history's oppressed peoples. What's odd about the desire of the British to make fools of themselves is that, historically speaking, they've done it from a position of strength.

After all, for about one hundred of Mr Punch's 147 years, Britannia ruled the waves, not to mention roughly one-third of all the *terra firma*. Since then we've slid down the table of the league of nations, so we've had plenty to be self-deprecating about. And it's true to say that when Britain is at its weakest – the early '40s, or the early '70s, for example – its humour, as displayed in the pages of *Punch*, is at its very strongest. But we wouldn't have taken so happily to disaster if it didn't suit our national characteristics; our sense of irony, for example, or that typical British determination not to take things Too Seriously.

You only realise how deep those habits go when you meet other people. Take Americans. Now they are Terribly, Terribly Serious. Your average American has a perfectly good sense of humour, which he or she uses when watching *Cheers*, or standing in line for Police Academy 23. The American Sense of Humour, however, has absolutely nothing to do with serious things like making money, or working hard, or consulting one's personal dietitian. A British person would find it hard to refer to any of these activities without some sort of jokey remark, since it wouldn't be right – even after a decade of Mrs T – to be seen to be trying too hard. An American would not confuse his conversation partners by adding inappropriate humour; for them it wouldn't be right *not* to be seen to be trying too hard.

This explains both why America is so much more successful than Britain and why Britain is still (just) a nicer place to live. Note the '(just)'; it's a little suggestion, an implication, perhaps, of the fact that things are getting worse and that – given half a chance – I wouldn't mind complaining about it. How British can you get? That sense of doom and gloom; that craving for a good whinge – trawl through the back numbers of *Punch* and you will find a rich seam of moaning made humorous.

What's wonderful is that we always go on about the same old things. These days there's a weekly feature in *Punch* called 'Even Now'. It's a reprint of an old cartoon picked for its contemporary relevance. I need hardly tell you that we are spoiled for choice. The Channel Tunnel, British Rail, polluted water, poisonous cheese, sex scandals in the Conservative Party, animal rights, medical wrongs ... you name the issue and *Punch* has had something to say on it. In all probability it's had something to say on it for a century or more. And just to cap it all, what it had to say makes just as much sense now as it did then.

The thing is, just to be French about it, *plus ça change, plus ce sont les mêmes Brits*. Just look at the subjects covered by the writers and cartoonists in this book; the Royal Family, snobbery, English food, animals (our love of, as compared with our mistrust for such things as, say, Art, or neighbours. Not *Neighbours*. We love *Neighbours*, although that, thank God, has not always been a part of our culture.)

Then run an eye down the list of the pieces and their creators. Pretty impressive, no? I mean, quite apart from all the certifiable superstars, like your Wodehouses and your Noël Cowards, what's amazing about *Punch* is how it has been the seedbed for so many funny ideas that have gone on to have a life of their own, to become part of our national culture.

The magnificent horror that is the life and spelling of Nigel Molesworth was first revealed to the world in *Punch*, 1939. It's hard to decide which was the more terrifying – Molesworth, or the Blitz. Mr Punch seems to have a penchant for ghastly children and their interests, Thelwell's demonic pony-clubbers, for instance, or the warped history lessons of *1066 And All That*.

They're all in this sumptuous volume, which makes, incidentally, an ideal Christmas present for that awkward godson or eminently forgettable auntie. You are that eminently forgettable auntie? I'm so sorry. I forgot.

Anyway, they're all here, in living monochrome and just as the title suggests . . . Utterly British. And utterly, utterly hilarious.

1

CLASS CONSCIOUS

'DO YOU KNOW THAT WOMAN?'
'ONLY TO TALK ABOUT.'

Alan Brien

TEST YOUR CLASS APPEAL

Just how classy are you, or that certain important person in your life? Too many readers these days still worry about whether they have a social role. Just remember that everybody, but everybody, has a class, and each class appeals to somebody, though not necessarily to the body who has it. Every class is exotic in its own way. The green is always grassier on the other side of the clubhouse.

In an article like this, of course, it is only possible to deal with broad specifications, such as working class, middle class and upper class. If you want a more detailed breakdown of your place in the pecking order, please complete this questionnaire, cut out the coupon on page 54 and post them to me with a week's income, and I will send you a more detailed analysis in a plain envelope.

Some clues to keep in mind. To the working class, the middle class often appear upper class. Many lively lads used to deceive themselves into thinking that they have married into the aristocracy simply because the wife's father has a house with gravel on the six-foot-long drive, a name on the gate, and a heated towel rail in the bathroom. The middle class almost never want to be working class or upper class, but many of them like to imagine that their ancestors were. The upper class would rather be mistaken for working class than middle class but are usually confident that they are above class of any kind.

On socially mixed occasions, one way of sorting out classmates is by listening to the JOKES they tell. Here are three typical opening lines.

1 'There was this Irishman, this Scotsman and this Jew ...'
2 'Apparently Parnell, Robert Louis Stevenson and Disraeli once met together and ...'
3 'An awfully funny thing happened the other day to three members of my club ...'
(This is an easy one – 1 is W, 2 M and 3 U)

Working class jokes are always immediately identified as jokes, and are concerned with types all of whom appear in a bad light. Middle class jokes will hope to pass as historical or cultural anecdotes and confuse any listener who does not know that Parnell was Irish. Upper class jokes are almost invariably presented as descriptions of events which actually occurred recently to some colleague, old schoolfriend or, preferably, relative of the teller. All upper class persons are cousins of all other upper class persons.

Another sign of class can be found in how the subject refers to his RELATIVES, especially his children. If you ask after his offspring, you will be told:

1 'Justin is a fine little chap and Amantha is awfully sweet.'
2 'Young Bert is a right little sod.'
3 'Who?'
(1 is M, 2 W, and 3 U)

You can often sort out class allegiances by sources of INFORMATION. An item of news, for instance, was obtained:

1 'On the wireless.'
2 'On the telly.'
3 'On the colour box.'
(1 is U, 2 W, and 3 M)

What newspapers are read by the subject, or at least bought?

1 News of the World, Mirror/Sun, Evening News.

2 Sunday Telegraph, Mail/Express, Evening News.
3 News of the World, Mirror/Sun, Times.
(1 is W, 2 M, and 3 U)

There is some overlapping here, and complete accuracy cannot be guaranteed. But one certain sign of upper classes in London is having the Evening Standard delivered to the house.

An insight into class ought to be MONEY but the amount available in ready cash is not an absolute guide. Try asking for a loan. Is the answer:
1 'Neither a borrower nor a lender be for the loan oft loses both itself and friend.'
2 'What's the damage?'
3 'I'd like to help but my trustees are terribly sticky these days.'
(1 is M, 2 is W, and 3 U)

CARS are a topic upon which all classes will be happy to give a specimen of typical conversation. Does the subject say:
1 'It's just an old banger.'
2 'It's a 1973 Ford Majorca GT de luxe with heated de-misting fast-back rear window, genuine leather steering cover, and automatic lighter on the walnut fascia.'
3 'It's just an old banger.'
(If the 'old banger' is a 1938 Popular then the respondent is W. If it is a 1964 Rolls, then U. But 2 is always M)

HOLIDAYS are another opportunity for the release of typical samples of boring evidence. But the catch here, I ought to warn the reader, is the upper class never have holidays. So perhaps we should eliminate 1 and 2 immediately.
1 'We are going away for a few weeks in the spring just wandering around Uttar Pradesh.'
2 'Some friends, my cousins actually, have offered us their *Schloss* in the Black Forest for the autumn.'
But 3 and 4 reveal basic class attitudes.
3 'We had 11 and a half days in Benidorm the year before last.'

4 'I haven't had a day to myself for 10 years.'
(3 is W, 4 M)

The WAR was a time when all classes submerged their envies and antagonisms in the struggle for democracy and fair shares for all. But looking back on the experience, attitudes vary. Who is most likely to reminisce:
1 'Jerry can't be trusted any more now than he could in the desert.'
2 'I was lucky to have a good war. Your German fights a good fight.'
3 'Despite everything, you know, my cousins kept the *Schloss* going through it all.'
(1 is W, 2 M and 3 U.)

NAMES are a useful pointer to class. Upper class members have a higher proportion of hyphens, twice as many Christian names, and usually sound like railway halts on a disused branch line in the hunting counties. But it is how you are addressed by whom which charts the subtler relationships. You are John Bertram Doe. Are you called:
1 'Mr Doe.'
2 'Young Bertie' or 'old J.B.'
3 'Young Johnny' or 'old Doe.'
4 'Bertram' or 'Doe.'
(If 1, then you are a M addressed by a W, or a M by a U. If 2, then you are M among M, depending on your age. If 3, then you are W addressed by U. If 4, then you are U talking to U, depending on whether you went to school with the speaker, or to a lesser school with his cousins.)

The approach to CELEBRITIES is also symptomatic of class background.
You can say:
1 'I believe we met once briefly at a party.'
2 'I saw you once on the telly.'
3 'You haven't changed a bit since I saw you at Fiona's wedding/Eddy Loamshire's memorial service.'
(1 is M, 2 W and 3 U)

SERVANTS are no longer the pointer they once were. Indeed, the word is never used by the working class who never had them and do not need them – the W male has his wife and mother to service him, the wife the children or the lodger, the children the mother or the aunty. W family structure is a form of group servitude. The M couple once had them, and like to pretend that they could still call on them if they weren't too busy being the backbone of the community, so they cling to the term. The U male or female still have them, but like to pretend that they are sharing them as a contribution to the national economy, and so rarely now use the word. Who will say:

1 'If you've finished laying the table, nip down to the corner for some fags before I finish reading the paper.'
2 'We don't run to a chauffeur but the butler sometimes drives me into town.'
3 'The servants were awfully amused at Benedict's knighthood – the au pair laughed and the cleaning woman always jokes about it when she comes on Mondays, Wednesdays and Fridays.'

(1 is W, 2 U and 3 M)

The principles underlying the structure should now be apparent. The upper class never boast about their privileges, but these are always in the plural. They always have 'horses,' and 'dogs,' and 'cars.' They refer to 'my doctors' and 'my solicitors' and 'my cousins.' (You might care to test yourself on who says 'the quack' and who 'the specialist down at the Infirmary'.) It is very middle class to cite the brand names, the models, the shops where you have an account. (Who would say 'There were three wines with the meal,' and who 'they gave us quite a decent plonk,' and who 'actually it was Château Mon Repos 1946 which couldn't have cost less than a fiver a bottle'?) The working class are awed and apprehensive about almost anything that happens to them. The middle class are outspoken and indignant about the things which don't happen to them any more. Nothing happens to the upper class. They are what happens to us, unless we watch out.

January 1973

'Lionel claims to be the only white hunter living in Surbiton.'

'Now look, son – anyone who isn't sure whether he's upper, upper-middle, middle, lower-middle or working-class is invariably lower-middle.'

'Class snob me foot. Just happens it's the only paper in the waste baskets of the offices I clean.'

David Langdon

TOUCH OF CLASS

'Has this fascinating ability to switch accents according to the class of customer.'

'On "Good Morning" terms until I discovered he was a junior executive at BR with a free rail warrant.'

'Things **are** changing. Years ago we'd have blackballed you as property tycoon. Now we just say there's a waiting list.'

THE HEIGHT OF IMPROPRIETY

Miss Grundison, Junior. 'THERE GOES LUCY HOLROYD, ALL ALONE IN A BOAT WITH YOUNG SNIPSON AS USUAL! SO IMPRUDENT OF THEM!'
Her Elder Sister. 'YES; HOW SHOCKING IF THEY WERE UPSET AND DROWNED – WITHOUT A CHAPERON, YOU KNOW!'

Richard Gordon

THE OTHER SIDE OF THE FENCE

Winston Churchill was still Prime Minister when we left the trendy treeless streets for the almond-blossom punctured pavements of suburbia. Everyone round us played tennis. All afternoon came the jolly *ping*, the wild cries of exultation, the breathless moans of despair, that would have fitted the soundtrack of a blue movie.

In the 1960s they built houses on the tennis courts. In the 1970s they built houses in the gardens of those houses, filling the serving-courts. In the 1980s, whole families are accommodated in the side-lines. We have become a neighbourhood.

We hate neighbours, as Sir Clifford Chatterley hated gamekeepers.

This is unChristian, but the injunction to love them as ourselves was uttered on the coast of Judaea, which at the time contained four small, scattered settlements in 40 Roman miles.

The knot of neighbourhood is complex. It barely deranges our suburban way of life. We can watch television three houses away through the picture windows. In autumn our suburb reeks like Dickensian London, as we burn our sedately swept leaves. (The *Financial Times* is a superb incinerator, you can tell a suburb is doing well by the charred pink fragments of Stock Exchange prices skipping along the paving-stones in the equinoctial gales.)

Our neighbours' L-plated teenagers practise reversing between our gateposts. Our neighbours' dogs, so inhibited by our Council's constipating pavements they clearly suffer from Freudian anal eroticism, in the gutter beyond our privet joyfully – as we put it in suburbia – perform their toilets.

We overhear the teasing chatter of decorous Sunday morning drinks on neighbouring patios, the playful splash in puddle-sized pools, the popping of motor-mowers, the teeth-gnashing of hedgecutters, Terry Wogan and Simon Bates, the amputating screech of chain-saws, the impromptu peals of unreliable burglar alarms. We smell in summer the barbecued holocausts, all year the halitosis of extractor-fans, more adventurous supermarket packaging affording our English suburban gardens at eventide the exciting stinks of Hong Kong, Acapulco or Bombay.

The neighbours' washing no longer flaps on the lines like the signals on the Navy's yardarms, both functions being performed out of sight through the miracles of modern technology. The golf-balls our neighbours slice against our windows are friendly soft plastic. Their children no longer play raucous soccer on the lawn, they silently repulse space invaders indoors.

In the warmhearted North – I hear – they constantly leave the holystoned front steps of their terraced houses to borrow a tin of treacle from their neighbours. In the South, we never borrow even a political opinion from ours. We nod at each other, speechlessly polite. Our dinner guests are other people's neighbours. We never marry neighbours. We die in the neighbourhood hospital and are buried invisibly by Francis Chappell. We never send neighbourly Christmas cards. We are no trouble to each other.

We hate our neighbours because, as obviously as Everest, they are there.

We all escaped from the crammed and garish city to its spacious fringes, tangy with lawn fertiliser, prim with laurel, tasteful with garden statuary and peppered with Green Line bus stops, because we craved an existence unshadowed by anyone else's. We overlooked that each city's suburbs grope for another's as instinctively as the fingers of lovers, and the English shires are largely reduced to the motorway verges.

We suffer neither resentment nor envy nor suspicion at the life-style of our neighbours. Just bafflement.

Why do they fit their suburban homes with Cotswold front doors and farmhouse kitchens, block the windows with vast shiny green plants and floodlight the garden? What do they think about, hour after hour near-naked and motionless on the recliner in the sunshine? Do they jog only to sport a sexy tracksuit? Do they bike to the station to keep fit, or has the HP foreclosed on the car? Did they buy a Range Rover because our tarmac is occasionally slushy, or to indicate rugged roots in the broad acres? Did they buy a Rolls out of modesty, to make their house look even smaller? Are the rousing chimes as the dustmen empty their bins the clash of empty gin bottles?

In the still of the small hours, when Southern Region hushes its busy chatter, the police cars briefly eschew their posthorns, the air is empty of whooshing jets, we sometimes wake in our fully-fitted bedrooms, pitch dark but for the green glow of the digital hour, and contemplate with a mixture of marvel and repulsion our neighbours in horizontal pairs all round, thick as kippers on a fishmonger's slab.

Tender is the night, even in suburbia. What are they getting up to, under their dreamy duvets amid the free-standing suites of their own bedrooms? This makes us eye each other the next day, as we go about our seemly tasks of cleaning the car and Hoovering the lounge, with the irrepressible curiosity of fellow-guests at a packed honeymoon hotel.

To pretend our neighbours do not exist, we supplement the neighbourly interface of a featherboard fence with the invaluable *Cupressocyparis leylandii* from our neighbourhood garden centre.

This bluish-green hybrid cypress, resembling a steamrollered Christmas tree, enjoys amazing growth in the stoniest soils and bleakest sites. It shoots up a yard a year, almost 6 inches every July. With a little

patience, our neighbours will softly and suddenly vanish away, particularly as they have energetically planted as many Leyland Cypresses to lose sight of us. From our attic windows, our suburb resembles the rainforests of the Amazon.

Our neighbours are still increasing in our neighbours' gardens as steadily as a colony of reproducing bacteria. These simply repeatedly split in two. As the world population is predicted to double in the next 50 years, the neighbourliness will become oppressive unless the real bacteria mercifully intervene. The plagues of the Middle Ages were wonderful for keeping population at socially acceptable levels. The Lord had nothing to spoil the extensive views from his Manor, save intrusive villeins swinging from his gibbets.

I am shortly standing for our suburban Council with the slogan, 'Bring Back the Black Death!' It will do marvels for the rush hour traffic, too.

April 1984

'They'll be unbearable when they get the swimming-pool.

John Cleese

JUST GOOD FRIENDS

I am glad to say that I have a lot of friends including Ian Fordyce (TV Producer), Michael and Helen Fipp's', Nicholas Walt, Mr Bailey and many others.

I do not need to name them all in this 'article' but I have a great deal of them (almost *too* many in fact!) although I pride myself I do not make a fetish about it, like for instance some people make out huge lists of 'Friends' and leave them lying around on the coffee table, pretending they had intended to put them in a drawer but had forgotten to do so in the rush, just to rattle you, but I usually find that half the names, if you press the point, turn out to be people they've just asked information from at information bureaus and then copied their names down from the plastic things they have their names printed on which they have on the counters in front of them when you ask them for the information, or even floor-walkers in Selfridges and people like that who must have badges pinned to them.

These names get quite easy to spot after a while, for instance if any of your friends' lists have 'E. W. Newell' on them, he is the man who gives information at King's Cross and 'Miss B. Sagar' was the lady in charge of Soft Toys at Derry and Toms before they closed. I actually know someone who once saw the name of the Fortnum and Mason Pie Department Assistant Manager on the friend-list of a famous Station Master! And he doesn't even wear a badge so he must have looked him up in *Who's Who* or somewhere!

Incidentally, if any of you spot names on your friends' lists that look suspect I can easily check them for you. I could find out and then you could come round to dinner if you were free, any time really, I'm usually in, and I could give you the details. You could leave when you wanted to, I'm not one of those people who get nasty when you want to go a bit early because you have to be up in the morning. I mean, just for an example, suppose the conversation *has* finally died, or the veal-and-ham *was* a bit off, it's always better to accept the rebuff gracefully, I always say, and show your guest out with a smile, than get involved in a scuffle with him. Not that it's even been a problem with me but I've seen people lose more, well, *potential* friends by oversensitivity in the early stages than by anything except strong religious feelings. Anyway do think it over, there's always room for one more!

Anyway, as I was saying, I believe that one's friend-list should only include one's real friends and acquaintances, for example, I could easily have written down Malcolm Kerr but I haven't seen him for quite a bit and I don't think it's really fair to say someone's a friend if you haven't seen them for *that* long, although he is really. I don't think you should include *anyone* you haven't seen for, say, ten years, *unless* they've been away and only then really if they've written at least once. (Unless things have been absolutely hectic for them.) And also you shouldn't put down people either who were friends once but definitely aren't any more. Mr Bailey does this, although he admittedly puts them under a special heading, but I say this is cheating although the Fipp's' think it's O.K. if you make it clear that they're not *good* friends. Well! That makes the whole *point* of the thing ridiculous. I mean *I* haven't put down Alan Hutchison, although he was my best friend until May 22nd last year, because you can't call somebody *any* variety of friend after you've had a scrap as prolonged as ours, particularly when it was his fault to start with. I mean we'd always got on very well, because we had the same number of friends on our lists. (Or very nearly, he always had one or two more than me but it's stupid harbouring a grudge about a small difference like that.)

But then *when* we agreed to pool all our friends, which was a brilliant idea because we both doubled our total, but which was *his* idea, I discovered, *after* the whole deal was finished and the agreement signed (and witnessed by Mr Bailey), that over half of his list (3 out of 5) were actually dead! He's not even copied them out of the street directory, he'd just taken them off tombstones! So he'd gained six real ones from me (or five anyway because I admit Sir Alf Ramsey was debatable) while I'd only got two from him, so that from really being 5–2 down he was now 7 all. He'd tricked me all along so that he could do the deal and get level.

I mean if he'd taken them out of the street directory I'd have spotted it eventually because you get to know those names after

THE BRITISH CHARACTER
LOVE OF KEEPING CALM

you've been at it a few years, but off *graves!* I honestly never thought anyone could stoop to that, and I said so, quite straight, and then he said that *my* friends might just as well be dead for all the use they were to anyone, and I asked him what he meant by that, and he said they were disturbed to a man, and that even Mr Bailey, who was once a teacher, had written the wrong name down when we asked him to sign the agreement, and that the Fipp's' were after me for what they could get, and that it was Nicholas Walt who had trodden on my hamster (to get even with me for my accident with his) and not the gasman, and I said the Fipp's' were a charming

couple, and he said what about the suggestions they had made to me, and I said that while I did not fully concur with all their views about the physical side of friendship, the essence of true companionship was the toleration of views abhorrent to oneself, and that Nicholas was *not* a spiteful man (though actually he is) (it had never occurred to me about Winston but it had the ring of truth) and, I said, what about Mr Fordyce, my TV producer friend, who directed many dramas we had all watched together at my place, and Alan said that he had emigrated in 1967 and had asked him not to tell me where.

This was a lie actually, but I fell for it

'For instance – obviously you haven't done under THIS bed.'

because we *had* been out of touch, and so, to cut a long story short, an awful fracas took place. Anyway, I'll tell you all the details when you come round for a bite to eat, next week is good for me, most weeks are O.K. actually, just drop in any time really, except I usually go for a bit of a walk about 3 a.m.

So see you next week if you can make it, and you can go when you want, as I said. Incidentally if Malcolm Kerr reads this do give me a call, I'd love a cup of tea or even a game of squash. I've improved a lot since the last time we played.

February 1973

Mary Dunn

(Blanche Addle of Eigg)

THE MEMOIRS OF MIPSIE

COMING OUT

What an auspicious event this was in the good old days, and how different from the present time, when a girl's figure scarcely changes with her début and young people seem old before their teens! 'Do you mind awfully if I cut Lord's this afternoon, grandpapa?' my grandson said to Addle just before the war at the Eton and Harrow. 'There's a new film I want to see.' I was somewhat shocked, I must confess, but Addle said nothing. Indeed, he is inclined to be taciturn during a cricket match, I have noticed, and often his only remark during a whole day is 'Wait till the end of the over, dear.' (I suppose he thinks, in his old-world courteous way, that the players would have to stop their game if I get up from my seat. He is always so considerate.) I am very fond of watching cricket myself, when with a cushion and a congenial companion one can spend the pleasantest afternoon, chatting of times past and present.

To return to girls' figures in the eighties, what miracles of elegance and womanliness they were! The tiny waist, the soft curves above and below, the smart bustle behind. I must admit, though, that the right effect was not achieved without trouble and sometimes tears. Gone were the days my mother knew, when she used to lie on the floor while an exceptionally strong footman (blindfolded of course) used to place one foot in the small of her back and lace her up. But a figure was still sufficiently important in 1889 for Elsie Rye (Lord Peckham's elder daughter) on the even of her coming-out ball, to get her young sister to hammer in a croquet hoop round her waist while she lay on the lawn. Unfortunately the sister was then called in to bed and poor Elsie lay the whole night pinned to the damp grass and had pneumonia next morning. Another friend, Lady Mary Linsey-Wolsey, who had the misfortune to be very flat-chested, bethought her of wearing an air cushion inside her dress; but in the crush of a reception she unwisely mounted a chair – someone's hat-pin punctured the air cushion, and the whole crowd looked on in horror while her corsage collapsed with a long whine.

Another trial was hair. Fashion demanded a hair style which needed great luxuriance of woman's glory, and although of course we Coots all had beautiful hair, others were not so blessed, and were forced to wear false switches or coils pinned on. (I hope my male readers will not be shocked to hear of this deception!) My cousin Clara Twynge was very unlucky in the management of hers. They kept slipping off, once into the offertory plate, and once into a jug of fruit-cup at a ball, which added somewhat to her natural shyness. Indeed, between that and the fact that she was distinctly plain (I do not know why, for she was a close cousin of ours) she was scarcely ever asked for a dance, and some unkind girls dubbed her 'Cloakroom Clara' because she used to spend almost every evening in that sad spot. Eventually Mipsie heard of this, and with her usual warm-hearted sympathy soon put things to rights. At the next ball, when Clara entered the ballroom, all eyes were drawn to a card attached to her bustle: 'Still waters run deep.' That evening she was besieged with partners and received three offers of marriage, all of which, in her shyness, she accepted, which was fortunate as two of the suitors threw her over next morning.

Even in that age of beautiful women Mipsie's entrance into Society created something of a sensation. '*Qui est cette demoiselle là?*' asked the French Ambassador, a great connoisseur of beauty. When informed he said simply '*Tiens!*' and continued to look at Mipsie. Even his Gallic eloquence was silenced by such loveliness, it seems. The same evening HRH the Prince of Wales – afterwards King Edward VII – was evidently much struck with her. She happened, in the supper room, to drop her fan almost at his feet. In a flash he had picked it up and handed it to her. A few minutes later she tripped on the staircase (she trips very easily, I have often noticed) and his was the hand that came to her rescue. 'You are unfortunate this evening, Lady Millicent,' the Prince said gravely, while Mipsie blushed vividly at the compliment implied. A royal memory for faces is well known of course, but Beauty in Distress had evidently made an indelible impression on her future Sovereign.

But, indeed, Mipsie was always the pet of royalty. Her flashing wit and brilliant repartee often saved some difficult situation and turned a frown from a royal brow. I remember one party at the Royal Yacht Squadron garden during Cowes Week, when the some-what austere King Crustatian of Iceland was the guest of honour. A sudden thunder shower had turned all the milk sour and HM was disposed to be annoyed, when: 'There shouldn't be any shortage of milk at *Cowes*,' said Mipsie audaciously. The royal displeasure suddenly melted into a smile, while everyone blessed Mipsie for the quick wit that relieved the tension.

On another occasion she was able to do great service to her country by saving an Eastern potentate from an embarrassing episode. During a house-party at the Duc de Tire-Bouchon's lovely château for the Chantilly races, the vastly rich Great Curd of Bokhara had ordered a beautiful butterfly brooch to be carried out in rubies, amethysts and emeralds, the Duc's racing colours, as a gift for the Duchesse. This lovely jewel was to be placed, as a charming whimsy, in a naturalistic manner amongst the flowers at dinner. But the jeweller had made a mistake and used sapphires instead of amethysts. There was a nervous pause while everyone looked at the butterfly and wondered what was wrong, for the Curd's face was like thunder. Then Mipsie, suddenly realising the situation, took the brooch and swept him a deep curtsey. 'I am honoured, your Highness,' she said, 'both by the gift and by your gracious memory of our armorial colours.' It was a brave, splendid lie (for the Briskett colours are red and silver), told so as to save a foreign Power from embarrassment. Relations were distinctly strained between our two countries at the time, so who knows what political strife, or worse, may have been averted by her noble action? But that is not the only time my dear sister, by her tact and brilliance, has helped her country, I am proud to say. At one time she was known as 'The Foreign Office Bag', so many statesmen and State secrets did she hold in the palm of her lovely hand.

March 1945

'That will be all for this evening, Barker.'

Tina Brown

VILLAGE FÊTES

Whereas the village fête was always a bum steer for my money – at the last moment Judith Chalmers invariably took a rain check on it, and we ended up with Ronald Colman's daughter or Leslie Howard's stepniece cutting the tape – the Fair was Something Else. Moony in the caterpillar, sick in the Whip, I thrilled to the flash yob with the quivering quiff who leapt between the Dodgems, gasped as one tentacle of Shaw's Continental Octopus whirled me out across the lights. 'If you don't believe in for-ever,' the Juke Box exulted, 'Then Life is Just a One Night Stand.'

The dud economy seems to have changed all that. This Summer the humblest village fêtes and bazaars are likely to be doing better business than the fair. There's a hectic quality, I noted, to the bowling for a pig, a wild extravagance to the surmise about the cake's weight. Rotary Clubs and Round Tables across the country are giving themselves strokes organising bigger and bolder Wellie Boot throwing competitions and knocking up ten pee a ride Dragons out of invalid cars and green sail cloth. It seems that the fête is no longer an occasion for trudging sullenly round the cricket pitch in a light drizzle with a tote bag full of damp Angel cake, plastic sandals and the four Dennis Wheatley novels you yourself donated the previous year. Inflation has made fund raisers of us all.

In the basement of the Cumberland Hotel on Sunday the febrile atmosphere of commerce at the May Bazaar could not entirely be disassociated from its sponsors, the Jewish National Fund. 'You, because I like you,

fifty pee,' announced one genial stall-holder, tossing me a Mickey Mouse toothbrush stand. Bettine Le Beau's opening speech was drowned in the rush for Spring Back foldaway chairs and shrewd patriots beating down the price of Ready Made Glitex curtains. 'Bendy Toys for all the Kiddies,' raved the intercom system. In a more chic corner I jostled among the nose-jobs for a bottle of cut-price Tabu perfume.

Compared to this excitement Crystal Palace Fun Fair was a tame business. A couple of morose tots dribbled round on aeroplanes and a few truant Hare Krishna disciples in sarongs and red woollen socks dangled plastic reticules for goldfish. Likewise the machines themselves looked in sorry nick. The Dodgem in which I chased a pimply tyke of seven was badly in need of an M.O.T. test and for twenty pee a crack the Palace of Ghosts was a potting shed haunted by a police klaxon.

'Hard lines,' cackled the lone hag at the Hoopla stall, pocketing my forty pee.

It's small wonder that the fairgrounds are feeling the draught. As Mr Frederick Gray, currently occupying the Vale of Health at Hampstead explained, with the tax man on one side and on the other the local authorities suddenly coming on conservationist it's a dead loss for today's showmen. 'We've offered three and four hundred quid for some village greens,' he fumed, 'but they still turn their noses up. Then they cut up ugly when we put a few pence on the Dodgems.'

The Grays, like the Ayres, the Bottoms and the Squire family have been in the fair business for generations. It irritates them when the public lump them in as gaudy vagrants with the tinkers and the gypsies. According to one of my sources – the Lover's Tunnel Operator at Battersea – the showman's moral standards are exceptionally high. They marry other fair families and stay married. They keep to their caravans and want no truck with the Flatties (house dwellers) of this world. Their lives, it seems, are inextricably bound up with their machines, a fact intriguingly borne out by the reports in the showmen's newspaper *World's Fair* which reads like a mechanised 'Jennifer's Diary'.

'At a North London fair,' we are told, 'there was George Furlborough's Fun Tower looking extremely impressive, T. Wilson's Flying Jumbos in new paint, Bert Cole's Rota, Charlie Edward's Twist, and, in bold partnership, Rose's Beach Buggy Dodgems and Maxwell's Spinning Waltzer.'

On first meeting, the showmen themselves are a taciturn breed with a dogged disinclination to come up with flamboyant quotes.

'It's just a matter of getting into a groove, see,' conceded the Big Wheel at Barham Park when I probed him about his Colourful Lifestyle.

'Isn't your job a bit embarrassing,' marvelled the Shove Halfpenny, 'going round fairs asking people daft questions all the time?'

One who was more eager to talk was seventy-three-year-old May Donaldson, in her time a travelling show-woman with such fairground greats as the late lamented Swaly Bolesworth. Now a reluctant flattie with a rented house in Battersea, she pines for the Bingo stall, rifle range and Tip the Lady out of Bed that she ran for twenty-five years in Battersea Park. Then, in her own phrase, 'along comes a lot of do-gooders in beards' who elected not to renew the showmen's lease and turfed them out of the park.

'There's no space for the old-timers now,' she told me, her small face dwarfed by a busby of platinum candyfloss. 'It's all right for the Rockets and the Dodgems but the sideshows have had it.'

Back at the Vale of Health Fred Gray confirmed her gloom.

'I want to say to some of these high and mighty politicians – Do you know how much it costs to run a Kiddie Copter?'

June 1976

'I feel such a fool standing in full evening dress on Victoria Station in the middle of the afternoon.'

THE MAN WHO ATE HIS LUNCHEON IN THE ROYAL ENCLOSURE

SCENE – *Drawing-room at Lady Dumpshire's. A ball in progress.*
He. 'No, I HARDLY EVER GO TO THESE PRIVATE DANCES. IT'S SUCH A NUISANCE HAVING TO BE ON ONE'S BEST BEHAVIOUR ALL THE TIME.'

Ned Sherrin and Caryl Brahms

REGRETFULLY YOURS ...

There is an industry in youthful indiscretion, a fine old trade handed down from father to son, British in concept, British in execution, yet because of the secrecy which is essential to success in this field, no recognition has been accorded, no honours bestowed, no Queen's Award for Industry handed out to the family who were pioneers and who, one thousand years on, are still the principal unsung practitioners.

The great founder of the Fitz-Wimble Strangeways family firm in A.D. 694 was one Will o'Wimbledon, an apparently simple, shock-haired lad living a rustic life on common land who had the foresight to hoard for years an illuminated letter from an obscure Durham monk, known at the time as the Vulnerable Bede. In the carefully delineated manuscript the Vulnerable Bede thanked Will for services rendered and enclosed in the parchment half a groat and a griddle cake. In a true flash of creative inspiration Will o'Wimbledon realised that, a man of the cloth, Vulnerable at 21 might well be Venerable by the time he was sixty and so with a little judicious blackmail he founded the family fortunes. A set of Bede's beads at first, then a silver chalice, 10 per cent of the Glebe one year, a plentiful supply of Bede's Mead the next; soon his little wattle hut began to bulge with the good things of Anglo-Saxon life.

The Dark Ages were exciting times for the family. Spreading the length and breadth of the kingdom, they soon had a finger in every fallible corner. Young women with an inclination for witchcraft, over-emotional minstrels, unstable pages, sensitive squires, anyone whose indiscretions might have led him to the ducking stool, the ordeal by fire or the hand summarily cut off, was grist to the family mill. The only thing that kept the family back was widespread illiteracy; but as soon as a man could make his mark he was a marked man.

With the Conquest the Wimbledon family immediately learnt to interpret Norman French and acquired the prefix 'de'. It was one Gui de Wimbledon (1154–1217) who accompanied Richard the Lionheart on the Crusades. The King's relationship with his minstrel Blondel had seemed an ideal Wimbledon gambit. Collections were made from all the cadet branches of the family to set up Gui with armour and equipage, Squire and page and to fit his lady, Guinevere de Wimbledon, who was being left behind, with a Chastity Belt. It was the first time that the de Wimbledons had attempted to cash in and cash up on a Royal Indiscretion.* They were playing for high stakes.

Unfortunately, they made one vital miscalculation. Since the King and Blondel communicated mainly in ballads which they accompanied on their own guitars, concrete evidence was impossible to acquire and six months' dusty travail in the Holy Land in daily danger of leprosy and Saracens yielded

only one indiscreet epistle from the Apostle Paul to an individual Corinthian on which it was too late to proceed; though on the journey home Gui de Wimbledon, returning via Rome, was able to use it to extract enough hush-money from the Pope to cover his expenses.

However, valuable lessons had been learnt by the time it came to dealing with Richard the Second and Edward the Second. The dangerous aspects of Royal Extortion were further demonstrated when Will Wimble (the family name was discreetly re-Anglicised during the Hundred Years War) turned up at Henry the Fifth's coronation with a packet of the new King's love-letters to Doll Tearsheet. Will's come-uppance took the form of immediate conscription to fight at Agincourt where Henry the Fifth saw to it that he was first unto the Breach and never heard of again. Fortunately for the family line he had already sired three progeny who continued to run their father's business discreetly and successfully.

The Wars of the Roses provided a bed of roses for the Wimbles. Caxton had by now invented the printing press, in many cases giving an even greater sense of permanence and authority to the evidence they were amassing. A slender volume of love poems could be almost as damaging as a straightforward letter if placed in the wrong hands.

By harking back to the primitive but undeniably effective methods of the founder of the family, the Wimbles scored heavily when it came to the Dissolution of the Monasteries, many of which were torn apart by angry parents incited by Wimble guile. At this time Wimble Abbey became the family seat from which Gervase Wimble (1493–1594) continued to ply the family trade which had by now escalated to the status of a well-respected profession.

Three of King Henry the Eighth's wives subscribed handsomely to the family coffers, justifying the recently-acquired family

---

* Nothing has been substantiated with regard to William Rufus.

motto: 'You never extorted it so good.' The reign of Queen Elizabeth was the Golden Age of Wimblery. All over England passion was rising, rhetoric was spouting and Courtly Love was in flower; and Courtly Love sounds just like any other sort of love when committed to paper by anyone who is less than a Master of the Language.

Lady Jane Grey, Mary Queen of Scots, Darnley, Bothwell, Rizzio, The Earls of Leicester and Essex, Raleigh and Sidney, as well as several assorted Spaniards put pen to paper so frequently and so rashly that the senior branch of the family was able to retire and devote itself to the more respectable professions of piracy and the slave trade. Their only failure was when Kit Wimble (1565–1632) confronted Shakespeare with letters from the Earl of Southampton, The Dark Lady of the Sonnets, Francis Bacon and Mr W.H., and threatened to show them to Anne Hathaway. Shakespeare declined to settle, murmuring: 'You can't have met my wife.' A modern Wimble is trying to sell them to Professor A. L. Rowse.

It was left to the Fitz-Wimbles, the bastard branch of the family, to carry on the threat. It was a Fitz-Wimble who became possessed of Guy Fawkes's instructions on how to blow up the Houses of Parliament ('Light the Blue Touch-paper and Stand Well Away'). The Fitz-Wimble Library still holds Lord Chesterfield's son's unfranked replies to his father's letters; and it was a Fitz-Wimble forgery that ruined the first night of *The Beggar's Opera* by suggesting that the play had made 'Gay rich and Rich gay', which was not the conventional thing to be in those days. Another Wimble earned a couplet – not one of his best – from Pope:

> Straight to the point as needle is to thimble,

> Hungry t'extort flies th'acquisitive Wimble.
>
> (*Rape of the Wimble*)

By now the Fitz-Wimbles were getting into Europe and beyond. There had been a Fitz-Wimble on the *Mayflower* with very little to show for it, and Fitz-Wimbles were sighted in the area on the occasion of the premature deaths of Byron, Keats and Shelley. Harriet Wilson, whom the Duke of Wellington told to 'publish and be damned', is now revealed as a Miss Fitz-Wimble. Castlereagh and the Bishop of Clogger both went to school with Fitz-Wimbles and it was one thing for Nelson to turn a blind eye on the Fitz-Wimbles; but believe us they had no intention of turning a blind eye on him or on Lady Hamilton.

Later in the nineteenth century, when hypocrisy afforded them a second Golden Age, Fitz-Wimbles encompassed the downfall of Dilke and Parnell and invented the Boy Scout Movement in an attempt (unsuccessful) to discredit Baden-Powell. Raschid el Fitz-Wimble served Lawrence of Arabia faithfully in Mesopotamia and Lloyd George conferred a Baronetcy on Sir Carstairs Fitz-Wimble Strangeways without the family having to fork out a penny.

A flourishing branch of the family emigrated to America in 1939 and controls many senior positions in the CIA. The South African branch of the family was well represented at the last annual re-union and the most recent sighting of a Fitz-Wimble at work has been in North Devon.

Floreat Wimble!
June 1976

'Good heavens, Lavinia! It says here the East Wing was burned down last night.'

David Taylor Talks to

SPIKE MILLIGAN

SPIKE MILLIGAN HURTS. A graffito. *Graffito, ergo sum.* To be sprayed in letters six feet high, This Side Up, the other side down. Possibly it's a neon sign, or illuminated, knee-on prayer stool. It could be a book. Spike writes something beginning with B, nearly 3 million paperbacks sold to date. Is that why I've come to see him? If only he were a scholar, if only he could spell. If only his tomatoes weren't green.

We're all a bit strange. His son is a bricklayer, did I know that? Maintains Spike's house and says he's a happy man. But how *can* they govern China? What, when we can't any longer all fit on to an area the size of the Isle of Wight?

Hitlergram Nummer Zwei!
HITLER: If only I had known.
GOEBBELS: If only you had known vat?
HITLER: *That's* vat I don't know.

Publish and be drubbed. Bring tea! Fetch cake! It's life that's probably to blame. He was born in India, once, now it's standing room only. Terence Alan Milligan, son of late Capt. L. A. Milligan, MSM, RA retd. Perhaps it was the heat.

The graffito might do on a tombstone one day, tombstone as big as The Ritz. SPIKE MILLIGAN HURT, or HURTED. Certainly his head hurts and, by the look of him now, there may be bodily hurts besides. They recently improved his eyesight, making it worse than it was and harder to paint. For him to paint. Not for them to paint his eyesight. Who'd want to paint that? Van Gogh's eye. Choice of blue or brown, please state when ordering, tick box if colour-blind.

It hurts when he laughs. It hurts when he cries. Spike, as ever, might well do either and very likely both, apparently on whim. Read *Guardian Whim*, every Tuesday.

Still, back meanwhile in reality, cut, zoom, SFX, I found it, then: the way to Hadley Common. And the stars. When he moved here, to a turreted suburban château in much sought-after area, near school and Barnet, own flush toilet, a neighbour didn't know him from Adam, and he didn't know Adam either. Till one fine day, with a *rat-a-tat-tat*, the neighbour is standing at the door.

'Mr Milligan,' says he, 'I've just seen you. On the television.'

That seemed to be that. Right he was, said Spike.

Moments later, the scene changes to the neighbour's door, with a *rat-a-tat-tat*, Spike standing without.

'Mr Neighbour,' says he, 'I've just seen you. In the garden.'

Quiet, please, let's have some hush. When you're ready, Spike, go on a green. Drumroll. And the next object is – a Qantas hello-person. A Qantas hello-person.

Spike calls up.

G'day, Qantas, would he hold a moment, please? ... *Tum-ti-tum-ti-tum, tum-ti-tum-ti-tum* ...

Sorry to keep him waiting ... *tum-ti-tum-ti-tum, tum-ti-tum-ti-tum* ...

AAARGH! The dreaded, accursed piped music strikes again!

Eventually, Spike's connected. Could they help him?

Just a moment, says Spike, would they hold on just a moment? *Yesterday, all our troubles seemed so far away* ...

Hello? Hello? This is Qantas, could they help him please?

Sorry to keep them waiting, answers Spike, one moment please ... *now it seems as though they're here to stay* ...

Click-brrrr.

Christ almighty, the stuff is everywhere:

dehumanising wallpaper music, supposedly to soothe, but in his case making Spike seethe.

As so much does: like cruelty, rapacity, environmental rape. Like smoking, Mrs Thatcher or neglecting cats. Like hype and insincerity, war, the Japanese, and fluoride in the water. Getting asked about The Goons. Getting asked if he's off his chump.

All can be in a day's work for manic, stinging letter-writing Spike. You have to protest, and laugh, and maybe cry. The abject helplessness hurts just the same. The dinosaurs have perished. More tea! Extra cakes! Australia here he comes. Hello, mum! Ninety-two and an Aussie at last. The BBC want him out there next month, for a documentary, and he'd stay if it weren't for his kids. To be followed by a pantomime. It's best when there's no control.

Spike's First Law Of Physics says: If anything can happen, it will. He'd like to have met Churchill, Van Gogh and Jesus Christ. But this constantly nagging ultra-sensitivity hurts, whatever the Snap-Out-Of-It, Have-An-Aspirin brigade may say. There's just bugger-all you can do about it. Quasimodo was stuck with his bump.

Spike used to think psychiatrists would make it all better, take these pills, he'd become Eric James. Sid James. People always want to talk about that – his depressions, mental anguish, underlying gloom. No one ever writes up his bronchitis, though, to which he's been a martyr time and again. *The cough beneath the clown – by Spike as told to Our Pulmonary Staff.* Who listens to clowns? Journalists very often can't. He'll put a paper bag on his head and shout Go Away! Eff off! Alas, they seldom do. More tea!

The other thing they always ask is when will Spike retire? To which the answer is of course bedtime, same as usual. He was 67 in April, but just made it in to the new tax year, which he's started so he'll finish.

PROCLAMATION! All persons should be made to wear a hat with their overdraft written on the front of it, initialled by the Queen. It'd help decide whose round it is.

Heavens! Look at the time. Bong! Bittersweet comic Spike Milligan was interviewed for *Punch* today. Bong! Twenty minutes into an earnest chat, no one had mentioned The Goons. In Part Two, Spike learns to walk and is packed off to school at the Convent of Jesus and Mary, Poona; Brothers de La Salle, Rangoon, and SE London Polytechnic, Lewisham. Bong! Later on, war breaks out.

And nostalgia grips. It doesn't take much. The well-stuffed diaries are to hand, fat albums of his life in photographs banked. The past is secure and peculiarly vivid, perhaps because of that. Craziness is permanent. Like jet-lag that's lasted sixty years. Shut your eyes and transfer, say, to the Italian front – forty years on you can still remember what the weather was like (not bad for the time of year). Look Milligan, says Major Startling Grope. The Sergeant says you aren't very good at your job. He's a liar, sir. I'm bloody useless at my job. I could lose us the war.

How did he ever get into this mess? To think he used to be a semi-skilled fitter, Woolwich Arsenal. The semi-skill was in taking two lengths of wire, straightening them out, linking them together and passing them on to the next bloke. They then disappeared for good. Spike at his best did fifty bits an hour. Call that a day's work? they'd ask. No, he'd reply, he thought he'd call it Rosalind.

Gags like that sustained The Goons (AT LAST! *New Readers and The Prince of Wales start here*). The Goons made him famous and wretched. The Goons could have lost him his sanity, his marriage, little things like that. It didn't make him *quite* so famous as some, at the time, when he did mind a bit. Now Sir Harry is retired and Peter is dead, Bentine is around here somewhere, try the teapot perhaps. And the weather's still not bad for the time of year. He's seen too many good things come to an agonising end. Especially life with his second wife Paddy, who died of cancer aged 43. Next person to wonder why Spike can't be funny all the time, please step this way.

Bong! Dateline Rome, 23 February 1945. Gunner Milligan, Offspring of an Irish King, D Battery, 56th Heavy Regiment, has hung up his trumpet. A grateful nation gives thanks . . .

It started with pains in my chest. I knew I had piles, but they had never reached this far up before. The Medical Officer made me strip.

'How long has it been like that?' he said.

'That's as long as it's ever been,' I replied.

He ran his stethoscope over my magnificent nine-stone body. 'Yes,' he concluded, 'you've definitely got pains in your chest. I can hear them quite clearly.'

'What do you think it is, sir?'

'It could be anything.'

Anything? A broken leg? Zeppelin Fever? Cow Pox? La Grippe? Lurgi?

'You play that wretched darkie music on your bugle, don't you?'

'Yes, sir.'

'You must give it up.'

'Why?'

'I hate it.' He goes on to say, 'It's straining your heart.'

Bloody idiot. It's 1985, I'm a hundred and nine, and I'm still playing the trumpet. He's dead.

'No, Harold, you must *not* wear a made-up tie. What you've got to do is to get one with—

A PLAIN BIT AT ONE END –

AND A MID-VICTORIAN FIGURE
AT THE OTHER –

AND THEN YOU'VE GOT TO –

TIE IT –

AND PULL IT –

AND TUG AT IT –

AND FIDDLE WITH IT –

UNTIL –

IT LOOKS MUCH MORE LIKE A
MADE-UP TIE THAN A MADE-
UP TIE COULD EVER LOOK.'

Much the same must be said about the peaches he's now spotted laid to rest round the bottom of that tree, in the garden (perfect spot for a tree) round the house which is huge and now managed by the new Mrs Milligan, formerly Shelagh Sinclair of The British Broadcasting Corporation, which God preserve, if for no other reason besides Radio 3, last outpost of civilised culture. Spike's chaotic London office has been managed more or less since time began by Yorkshire's redoubtable Norma Farnes. Give us the facts, Mr Punch.

The reason, or part of the reason, for Spike's vast house, by the way, is that he did well from the sale of his erstwhile more modest suburban semi, out of which he was bought because all the local drains met under it and they wanted to install a new system. End of Aside One. More tea, Sookey! If people are to follow this in detail, they must have tea. Quick-brew, though, drink up. *Thames At Six* are coming at five. There isn't a moment to lose! Hark! Horses approach! Tea for the crew – that's 57 with, 122 without sugar and no cakes without consultation. Cut!

That'll have to do. No time, perhaps as well, to tell you his favourite racialist jokes or The 101 Best and Only Limericks of Spike Milligan. No time to save the whales. No time to turn bleak about pain and death and pointlessness or even to have a go in his new little snow-white Rover, here Rover, made from a million million Japanese bits. More bits!

Time to go home, time to go home, Spike now is tired, it's time to go home. But wait! Bong! Darling, I am home! Bong! Any chance of a cup of tea? Spike Milligan, Fused Again, Hadley Common. Shuffles papers. Pockets biro. Dims lights. Get up and walks into wall. Cut.

September 1985

Percival Leigh

MR PIPS HIS DIARY

Wednesday, March 21st., 1849. To-night to an Evening Party with my Wife, to Sir Hilary Jinks's, whereunto we had been bidden to come at 10 of the Clock; for Sir Hilary and her Ladyship have taken to keeping rare Hours. Thereat was a goodly Company of about an hundred, and the Women all very fine, my Wife being in her last Year's Gown, which I am tired of, and do hate so see. We did fall to dancing Quadrilles, wherein I made one, and had for my Partner a comely Damsel, whom after the Dance was ended, did hand to a Sofa, and thereon sit me by her Side; but seeing my Wife looking hard at us, did presently make my Bow, and so away. Then to look on while some did dance the Polka, which did please me not much, for had beheld it better danced at the *Casino*, and do think it more suitable to such a Place than to a Drawing Room. The Young Fellows did take their Partners by the Waist, and these did lean upon the others' Shoulders, and with one Arm stretched out, and holding Hand in Hand, they did spin round the Room together. But, oh! to see the kicking up of Heels and stamping of them on the Ground, which did mightily remind me of *Jim Crow*. In truth, I am told that the Polka is but a Peasant's Hop, from Hungary, and now to think of Persons of Quality cutting such Capers! Sir Hilary to his Taste; but a Minuet for me at Home, with Gentlewomen, and a Polka with Milkmaids at a Maying or a Booth. Meanwhile the Servants did hand round Glasses of Negus, which was poor Stuff; and those who listed

MANNERS · AND · CVSTOMS · OF · Yᵉ ENGLYSHE · IN · 1849.   Nᵒ 2.

AN "AT HOME".   Yᵉ POLKA.

to Supper when they chose, in a side Room, off wretched Sandwiches of the size of the Triangles in EUCLID his *Geometry*, which did think shabby. Home in a Cab, at Two in the Morning, much wearied and little pleased; and on our way Home, spying a Tavern open, did go and get me a Pint of Beer, and the same to my Wife; for we were both athirst, and she in an ill-humour about the Beauty I had danced with, and I because of the bad Supper; and so very ill-contented to Bed.

March 1849

'Honestly, Miss Trumbull, I can't think why we fought so hard to keep the membership exclusively male.'

George Grossmith

THE DIARY OF A NOBODY

April 28. – At the office, the new and very young clerk PITT, who was very impudent to me a week or so ago, was late again. I told him it would be my duty to inform Mr PERKUPP, the principal. To my surprise PITT apologised most humbly and in a most gentlemanly fashion. I was unfeignedly pleased to notice this improvement in his manner towards me, and told him I would look over his unpunctuality. Passing down the room an hour later, I received a smart smack in the face from a rolled-up ball of hard foolscap. I turned round sharply, but all the clerks were apparently riveted to their work. I am not a rich man, but I would give half-a-sovereign to know whether that was thrown by accident or design. Went home early and bought some more enamel paint – black this time, and spent the evening touching up the fender, picture-frames, and an old pair of boots making them look as good as new. Also painted GOWING's walking-stick, which he left behind and made it look like ebony.

April 29, Sunday. – Woke up with a fearful headache and strong symptoms of a cold. CARRIE, with a perversity which is just like her, said it was 'painter's colic', and was the result of my having spent the last few days with my nose over a paint-pot. I told her firmly that I knew a great deal better what was the matter with me than she did. I had got a chill, and decided to have a bath as hot as I could bear it. Bath ready – could scarcely bear it so hot. I persevered, and got in; very hot, but very acceptable. I lay still for some time. On moving my hand above the surface of the water, I experienced the greatest fright I ever received in the whole course of my life, for imagine my horror on discovering my hand, as I thought, full of blood. My first thought was that I had ruptured an artery, and was bleeding to death, and should be discovered, later on, looking like a second MARAT, as I remember seeing him in Madame TUSSAUD's. My second thought was to ring the bell, but remembered there was no bell to ring. My third was, that it was nothing but the enamel paint, which had dissolved with the boiling water. I stepped out of the bath, perfectly red all over, resembling the Red Indians I have seen depicted at an East-End Theatre. I determined not to say a word to CARRIE, but to tell FARMERSON to come on Monday and paint the bath white.

April 30. – Perfectly astounded at receiving an invitation for CARRIE and myself from the Lord and Lady Mayoress to the Mansion House, to 'meet the Representatives of Trades and Commerce'. My heart beat like

that of a schoolboy's. CARRIE and I read the invitation over two or three times. I could scarcely eat my breakfast. I said – and I felt it from the bottom of my heart – 'CARRIE, darling, I was a proud man when I led you down the aisle of the church on our wedding-day; that pride will be equalled, if not surpassed, when I lead my dear pretty wife up to the Lord and Lady Mayoress at the Mansion House.' I saw the tears in CARRIE's eyes, and she said, 'CHARLIE, dear, it is *I* who have to be proud of you. And I am very, very proud of you. You have called me pretty, and as long as I am pretty in your eyes, I am happy. You, dear, old CHARLIE, are *not* handsome, but you are *good*, which is far more noble.' I gave her a kiss, and she said, 'I wonder if there will be any dancing? I have not danced with you for years.' I cannot tell what induced me to do it, but I seized her round the waist, and we were silly enough to be executing a wild kind of polka when SARAH entered, grinning, and said, 'There is a man, Mum, at the door who wants to know if you want any good coals.' Most annoyed at this. Spent the evening in answering, and tearing up again, the reply to the Mansion House, having left word with SARAH if GOWING or CUMMINGS called we were not at home. Must consult Mr PERKUPP how to answer the LORD MAYOR's invitation.

May 1. – CARRIE said, 'I should like to send mother the invitation to look at.' I consented as soon as I had answered it. I told Mr PERKUPP at the office with a feeling of pride, that we had received an invitation to the Mansion House, and he said, to my astonishment, that he himself gave in my name to the LORD MAYOR's Secretary. I felt this rather discounted the value of the invitation, but I thanked him, and in reply to me he described how I was to answer it. I felt the reply was too simple, but of course Mr PERKUPP knows best.

May 2. – Send my dress-coat and trousers to the little tailor's round the corner to have the creases taken out. Told GOWING not to call next Monday, as we were going to the Mansion House. Sent similar note to CUMMINGS.

May 3. – CARRIE went to Mrs JAMES, at Sutton, to consult about her dress for next Monday. While speaking incidentally to SPOTCH, one of our head clerks, about the Mansion House, he said, 'Oh, I'm asked, but don't think I shall go.' When a vulgar man like SPOTCH is asked, I feel my invitation is considerably discounted. In the evening, while I was out, the little tailor brought round my coat and trousers, and because SARAH had not a shilling to pay for the pressing, he took them away again.

July 1888

Libby Purves
DUNPOSIN'

An Englishman has only to open his front door to make another Englishman despise him.

Very nearly true; but in my anxiety to paraphrase Professor Higgins (good books do furnish a sentence) I made my compatriots sound perhaps a little over-tolerant. Let me rephrase that: an Englishman has *not even* to open his front door before a fellow-countryman slips into a slow sneer of con-

TRUE HUMILITY
Right Reverend Host. 'I'M AFRAID YOU'VE GOT A BAD EGG, MR JONES!'
The Curate. 'OH NO, MY LORD, I ASSURE YOU! PARTS OF IT ARE EXCELLENT!'

tempt. Frosted glass? Oh, replaced Stained Victorian? A *lacquered* brass knocker? Surely that fanlight-leading is fake? Honestly, some people … Then the bell plays a tune, and the visitor enters with a triumphant smile, having placed his social opponent without so much as a glance at the telephone-cosy, the patterned wall-to-wall, or the wrought iron Madonna hanging in smoochy black outline from the Delft Shelft.

Half the fun of style-consciousness in Britain lies in sheer, exhilarating mutual jeering. Only a fool or a masochist allows *The Observer* to bring a wide-angle lens and a soothing reporter round to anatomise 'A Room Of My Own'; the entire nation can transfer envy and dislike effortlessly the next Sabbath day from the unfortunate celebrity

to his video cabinet, his horrible china, pretentious collection of jade, naff desk diary, or whatever. Fear and loathing in Dunroamin.

It is not, in fact, possible to get it right. One class's pride is another's shame. Cleaning ladies tolerantly despise their employers' filthy middle-class kitchens, with all that cracked old china gathering dust on the pine dresser they can't even afford to cover with Formica; aristocratic Old Tories snigger at the Cecil Parkinsons' far-too-pristine silver spoons. The miserable *Guardian* classes are stuck uneasily between two stools: dismissed as grubby and wasteful by visiting artisans, while the precious, nervous, artistically sluttish young Vivienne-Westwood-clad chicerati giggle rudely at their genuine horsehair sofas and subdued Sanderson walls. The

'Forget the crêpe Suzette, Minchin – I'll have the rice-pudding.'

middle classes get nothing right; our Suffolk plumber fell about in hilarious abandon at the sight of the elegant taps we expected him to fit to ye farmhouse sinke – 'Woss chawd and freud mean, then?' – and both honest builders and stylish surveyor knocked us down a peg or two for saying we quite liked the bare bricks with the plaster off.

Friends, very modishly doing up an Edwardian brick palace handy for the Television Centre, got half their specially-designed late Victorian tiles up on the bathroom wall, only to have a passing electrician lean on the bath and sympathise kindly, 'Sod to get off, those horrible old tiles, mate, aren't they?' Devastating.

The middle-class disease – only now being recognised and pilloried as such – is a horribly ostentatious lack of shame. The principle, evolved back in the earnest early Seventies when the nightdress-case and the TV cabinet finally became *de trop*, is never to hide anything. It evolved partly from a romantic idea of the grubby British aristocracy in its faded country houses, and partly from whole-earthism. Hence the bread crock, the stripped dresser, the Real Fireplace, the clocks with real works keeping wildly unreal time; hence, later, the acres of exposed brickwork, the tubular hi-tech bunks for unisex children, and the aggressively frameless pictures held together with steel clips.

Once the lower-middles got the idea, and began buying up warehouses full of modern laquered pine and fake farmhouse clocks with quartz innards, the leading contingent began to panic, distressing everything in sight with bicycle-chains and acid and taking positive pride in the sight of bare threads in the carpet. My parents accidentally gained special brownie-points in this phase, for having a huge ancient Axminster bought second-hand from the British Embassy in Hamburg. It had a spectacularly bald patch near the fire 'where the typists' feet used

to go'. This hinted simultaneously at racy diplomatic connections, aristocratic insouciance about appearances, and an amusing thrift.

A few years ago you could get away with most things by murmuring, 'It is, above all, of course, our family *home*,' and so implying a soul above Hicks and Mlinaric. But now, as once before in the days of Harold and Vita and Cecil and Noël and Gertie, top style has moved remorselessly out of the hands of family men and women, and into that of the aforementioned slender and wimpish chicerati. *They* do not have Fisher-Price toys rolling unselfconsciously around beneath their awfully decent mahogany chiffoniers; they do not put up shelves stained with amusing green varnish at a budget price.

No; some of them live in studied bareness with one £4,000 Milanese chair facing a bunch of pampas grass in an inexpressibly beautiful trouvé pig-bucket; some anxiously mix sea salt and oven cleaner into the Dulux to give depth and texture to the skirting-board; quite a few are so horrified about being judged by their surroundings that they live secretly in hotels, only coming out for parties.

Peter York, leader of the new wave of frizzy-haired, anxiously undomesticated social observers, told a magazine recently that what he most wanted was 'a walk-in American larder-fridge', although – italics mine – '*I never have food in the house.*' This combines an artful exercise in oneupmanship with a total concealment of the real nature of his home. Had he said, 'I'd love a nice vase for me prize chrysanths,' or 'Divertimenti have these simply super Yugoslavian oyster-ramekins,' we'd have got him pinned down for contempt or envy. But no; space for a larder-fridge, yet no food in the house ... brilliantly, York eludes the pursuing voyeurs and remains as aloof and impeccable as if he lived in the New York Plaza and never ate in.

There is one other answer, of course, which defeats the sneering interior-freaks and the honest philistine alike. Attempt the newest mode: Haute Clutter. We have a friend who lives in a sumptuous Georgian house, and I have not the faintest idea how it is decorated. No wall is visible, for rank upon rank of pictures (I am not sure what any of them represents); no shelf reveals its nature beneath the groaning mass of Victorian bottles, paper models, old irons, old iron, hats, feathers, statuettes, wills, candles, pieces-of-eight, stuffed frogs, Frog stuff, and bits of Napoleon's braces. If the whole ensemble was in a working-class semi, or gypsy caravan, and was a little less *recherché* in its scope, the owner would either be dismissed as vulgar or committed to psychiatric care as a Confused Subject. As it is, she is fêted as a priestess of design, and pays her cleaning lady handsomely to wander, and wonder, around Aladdin's junkyard with a featherduster.

She is aiming at the ultimate defence. One day, no Englishman will be able to open the front door at all.

February 1984

'Shall we join the ladies?'

2

CULTURE VULTURES

'I don't know much about Art – but I do know what I like.'

David Taylor

HIM INDOORS

When living in a foreign field, says Sir Terence Conran – who in point of fact seldom does, but is just supposing – many an Englishman might long for a vision of that most characteristically English scene of domesticity – country house comfort.

Now what exactly should one infer from that?

Gosh, well, if one were pinned down, one probably would have to say that it is a traditional vision which, inside English country houses and cottages, has scarcely changed for a couple of centuries. One pictures an underlying simplicity and an air of understatement. Really it's not in the English nature to swank and we tend not to over-decorate or over-pattern in the same way as, for example, do the French. Our style, according to Sir Terence, is a heady combination of spare comforts and a pleasure in the eclectic. There might, moreover, be just the suggestion of neglect, a hint of shabbiness – for the English do so love to have their homes look properly worn in – don't they? – and to exude a kind of careless, lived-in cosiness.

Now that comes firstly, perhaps, from a lack of overall planning. One means that the English do not, as a rule, engage interior decorators at the drop of a trilby the way so many Americans do. Over here that's still considered a bit nouveau chi-chi, only for those with enormous houses and resources to match.

Secondly, supposes Sir Terence, the characteristic English cosiness, one might almost describe it as an ambience of inspired clutter, or, to take a fashion analogy, the *layered look*, comes from our national habit of collecting bits of things – dozens and dozens of different and much-treasured objects, knick-knacks, *stuff*. We've always had a weakness for that. Perhaps it is part of our history as travellers and traders. Sometimes we brought back boatloads of souvenirs, other times we brought back ideas on such a scale that they influenced almost everything, as when we had passions for the classical styles of Italy, Greece or Egypt, or got hooked on the patterns of India or the Orient. The Victorian era did, of course, see the height of this. But then the Arts and Crafts movement subsequently resurfaced and other influences, like that of the German *Bauhaus*, tended to steer the English style back towards its original essential simplicity – look at the comparative austerity of some 1930s design.

For at root, Sir Terence is persuaded, we do like to keep things simple – despite that other weakness to stash and, maybe, a corresponding effect that derives from what might be described as a national 'make-do-and-mend' mentality – don't chuck it out, refurbish it.

So, then, the vision of the English country house: it's simple, comfortable furniture, oak and painted pine for the well-to-do, plain finishes for the poorer. It's prettily sprigged and rosy fabrics. It's patterned rugs and carpets, a hint of woodsmoke, a gleam of silver or brass – all helping to camouflage and to deflect the mud from one's messy pets. In summary, it's an undemanding, uncommitted look which never actually surprises one, yet always manages to satisfy. And, quite honestly, it's not something one can achieve satisfactorily anywhere but in the English countryside.

Which is where Sir Terence Conran *does* spend as much of his time as one can spare. One tends to sit in one's greenhouse. It's *such* a pleasure to scuttle off from the corporate hothouse and into the horticultural ditto, often taking a mountain of work to process, and a little fresh white wine. One is afforded the telephone-free tranquillity to concentrate, create, reflect or conceptualise. Which must be a must, musn't it?

Not that one was actually born to this Reilly-like life. One was typically middle-class, Daddy an importer of something called gum copal. With hindsight, Sir Terence will acknowledge that school – Bryanston in Dorset – had the most tremendous influence, stressing the arts and visual awareness, and one had a super teacher who was a sculptor and who passed on to one's impressionable mind the tactile delights of making things. Mother, too, had a very good eye and a great interest in the creative process. In the 1930s, some of one's earliest memories are of a wonderful cream room with big, forgiving club sofas and terribly simple bits and pieces, *objets*, and probably simplicity, almost it's austerity, has appealed from that time. What used to be called 'below stairs' furnishing can still have tremendous charm. It is whether it is *well done*. There's nothing to sneer at in reproduction furniture, for example, provided it has been sensitively done. How things are made is paramount.

It was with furniture-making that work for Sir Terence began and fortune-making is what has subsequently developed. A determination to apply the principles of good design has, above all else, sustained one. The Conran Design Group was at first, in the 1950s, a terribly modest outfit, snapping up little jobs like smartening up a coffee bar, but bit by bit the clients became bigger and more numerous so that one felt quite quickly that one was on to something that was a real need and long overdue for development.

It wasn't until the mid-1960s that the first Habitat shop was designed. The aim was to provide a showcase for Conran-made furniture and to demonstrate besides that the display and merchandising of household products was at that time (the Swinging Sixties, after all) also in need of an imaginative tweak.

To begin with, it was an awful sweat to find suppliers with the remotest spark of design-awareness – by which Sir Terence says he means practicality of purpose combined with striking good looks and consumer appeal – but as the business grew and flourished it of course became easier to commission.

Now every weekday and, if Conran had his way, it would be all week-end, Sundays included, too, thousands rummage through the breezily-presented domestic merchandise of what's become a national chain of Habitat stores, on the look-out for a keenly-priced bit of Bauhaus or a bentwood rocker, tile-top tables or a fun-fabric Chesterfield, the dizziest of duvets, handwoven druggets, bright acrylic fittings for one's kitchen or the loo, stripped-pine this or cork-finished that.

Well, of course it has paid off and one does find that as a result the pressure seldom lets up. One means that, Good God, with Habitat and the recently swallowed Heal's, with the design consultancy, the Mothercare business, chairmanships hither and yon, it has become pretty hard work to be Terence and increasingly that means a big-business operator as much as an inspired designer. One supposes that one is obliged to accept the fact that one *has* become a sort of byword, been labelled a guru. Yet one isn't, by the longest of chalks, in conscious pursuit of any such status, please appreciate that, and in fact one has an uneasy suspicion of all journalists who do have this tendency to spotlight one.

Good surroundings and crisp design, products with integrity, concepts which cohere. These, do you see, are one's personal delights. One's business is to pass them on, to galvanise others, stimulate, give effect, in short, make it happen.

There's a tremendous buzz to be had from that. One actually understood next to bugger-all about the machinery of business take-overs until quite recently but, in that rather irritating way that one has, one did get tremendously interested in every detail. Well, yes, that *is* true of so much of one's attitude to life. Perhaps that is it – *detail*. Some, one supposes, might accuse one of meddlesome interest in the details of everything that's going on around one, but that is what one is stuck with, if you like, by virtue of having an eye for things. One just doesn't miss much.

Yet one does try so hard not to be too flamboyant. Determined simplicity, that air of understatement, is the thing, in business, in design, at home. It has worked for one. And it is terribly English.

April 1984

'WHAT *a time I had persuading Mr Dali to paint the second one to match.*'

Basil Boothroyd

DON'T SHOOT THE PIANO – IT'S DOING ITS BEST

I may be one of the few British pianists to have been applauded by a chef and three waiters in Sparta. It was towards the end of my 'Where's the piano?' period, which must have lost me a lot of friends in my time, and offended hosts of hostesses, trying to interest me in a little intellectual conversation when all I wanted was to make with my arrangement of *Dark Town Strutters* famed for waking the babies and sending the cat under the sofa. I know better now. The idea, fostered by a long-dead advertising campaign, that the man who can play the piano is guaranteed all the social life he can spare from being mooned over by the pick of the girls, needs a sterner revision than the one it's currently getting from the Piano Publicity Association, who will have to go on

THE BRITISH CHARACTER
FAILURE TO APPRECIATE GOOD MUSIC

vamping the till-ready for the nonce. Don't go away, though.

The standing ovation in Sparta, as I realised when the ouzo fumes had dispersed, was not for the quality of my playing, but for my achievement in making that piano play at all. Once, walking on the South Downs, I came on the inside – or action, as we musicians call it – of a concert grand propped against a five-barred gate. No, I don't know how it got there. Feel free to speculate. But even that played better, yielding up *Danny Boy* to the cows and skylarks by sheer pluck, if harpists will excuse the joke. I chose *Back to Sorrento* in Sparta, and when I found that the first three notes, which should go up, came down, even though played up, and that a simple scale had to be assembled by random selection over the whole keyboard, I accepted a challenge that would have left Artur Rubinstein at a loss. It took time, my wife unsticking the hammers

'Please stop – Land of Hope and Glory always makes me cry!'

with a fruit knife, but I believe it's still being talked about there.

Now, according to the Piano Publicity Association, again campaigning, 1,700,000 British pianos need tuning (no statistics released for the Peloponnese), and most of these have needed it so long that they're past it. Skirting any question of whether this is the best way to improve the piano's image among 1,700,000 owners who regard it as a display area for wedding photographs, abandoned drinks and African violets, I'd like to say that I'm not a bit surprised.

Pianist I knew, late for a band concert in Oldham – I hope this isn't all too cosmopolitan – I once played a piano in a pub in Skegness and a man who dropped his tankard in it got his hand caught and had to be cut free by firemen – this friend of mine, then, rushed straight on stage, plunged his fingers into the ivories, and got dead silence. It was a leaky theatre, and the man who always took the action out to dry in the boiler room between performances hadn't bothered to put it back. What upset my friend, who luckily wasn't doing his *Rustle of Spring* solo spot until after the interval, was that no one noticed. Never mind the audience, you don't expect much from them. But when the other boys in the band get through the whole of 'Light Cavalry' without missing you, it's time to go over to the trombone.

The incident well illustrates the low esteem in which the piano is held. You'll have noticed at the Festival Hall that it has to have its name painted on the side to shore up its self-confidence, a thing unknown to other instruments. Ever see a piccolo dangling a banner saying Boosey & Hawkes? It's true that the pianist has compensations. He

'We like the plot, Miss Austen, but all this effing and blinding will have to go.'

doesn't have to carry his instrument around with him. When he gets there, there it is ... and only a man pressed for time will fail to look inside, not only to see if it's complete, but to get out the fag-packets, broken strings of cheap beads, saxophonists' dirty yellow dusters and the like. After that, round the front, to see how many notes play two, and whether the chair provided has been left behind by a dwarf act and won't raise him as high as the keyhole.

I'm not now thinking of the Festival Hall, rather of the school or parish ditto, and similar musical venues long disowned by St Cecilia. Oh, yes, I've played pianos in my time when even the dancers at Farmers' Balls have winced and kept to the far end of the room. They've often been rich in scrollwork, silk fronts painted with birds, and candlesticks that buzz like a running saw in sympathy with the entire range below middle C.

But it is in his own home that the pianist is chiefly scorned and rejected, and never more so than when guests have begged him to play, and will keep at him until he does. In my experience, it's best to get it over. I make a show of opening an album of very old Beethoven, printed in enormous crotchets and inscribed 'Lottie Beeston, Chepstow, 1911', but I always give them *Bye-Bye Blackbird*, and they wouldn't know the difference if it was *Ave Maria* arranged for percussion only. One chord, and they're off, pouring themselves drinks, passing the fags, discussing the Industrial Relations Act through mouthfuls of my Twiglets, and ignoring me until I stop. 'Oh, don't stop', they then say, so I start again, and so do they. I don't say I'm a Barenboim (they don't, either) but the piano's all right. It should be. It's called 'The Mendelssohn'. I tune it myself, when I can find the pliers.

And what the Piano Publicity Association can do, if they want a good word said for them in places where it will do the most good, is come round and hear me some time.

What the British piano needs is a little attention and applause.

Damn it, even in Sparta you get that.

August 1972

Miles Kington

EXCLUSIVE – FOUR UNPUBLISHED EARLY MASTERPIECES

THE CASE OF THE MISSING NAVY

Conan Doyle's first story (age thirteen)

'What do you make of this, Watson?' said Holmes, throwing a paper dart at me across the room. I unfolded it and saw that it was a letter.

'It has a message of some sort written on it,' I said. 'Gosh! Is this a new case?'

'Read it and find out,' said Holmes, filling his mouth full of the liquorice all-sorts which he always stuffed himself with when he was hot on the scent of another villain.

'WATSON IS GETTING TOO BIG FOR HIS BOOTS,' it said. 'WE SHALL GET HIM.'

'Well,' I said, 'I would deduce that it has been written by someone who thinks that I am getting too big for my boots and they are going to get...'

At that moment the door burst open and in came Queen Victoria, the Prime Minister, the First Lord of the Admiralty and several crowned heads of Europe. They were all disguised.

'Please sit down ... Your Majesty,' said Holmes. 'Have an all-sort.'

The Queen gasped.

'You recognised me!'

Holmes smiled.

'I could not help noticing the little marks on your forehead, which can only be caused by a crown. Perhaps you have read my essay on "Marks made by Hats". You are not the Kaiser, therefore...'

They all gasped.

'Wow, you certainly have an incredible gift for deduction,' said the Prime Minister. 'But let us get on with the story. We are in great trouble, Mr Holmes. The First Lord of the Admiralty has reported that the British Navy has vanished. If some German spy sneaks on us to the Kaiser, it could mean the end of civilisation as we know it, or at least it could mean the German Navy coming and shooting our holidaymakers.'

'Have *all* the ships gone?' said Holmes to the First Lord of the Admiralty, his keen eyes (Holmes's eyes, I mean) looking out from under his keen eyebrows. 'Even the Zeus class destroyers with twin fourteen-inch turrets?'

'Unfortunately are they all disappeared,' said the First Lord. With one stride, and then another one, Holmes leapt forward and pulled the moustache, beard, spectacles, hat and false nose from his face.

'Gentlemen,' said Holmes, 'Otto von Krempel, the German spy!'

      ★   ★   ★

'But how did you know?' I asked Holmes later.

'Jolly easy,' said Holmes. 'Any chap knows that Zeus class destroyers have a sixteen-inch

turret, also he spoke in a German accent. I am writing an essay on German accents. They only have one, the Umlaut. I thought of that joke this morning.'

'One thing more.'

'Yes?'

'Who wrote that threatening letter to me?'

'Who do you think?' said Holmes, throwing a cushion at my head.

DEATH AT TEA TIME

Ernest Hemingway's first story (14 years old)

Haley went out into the school yard. The first leaves of autumn were falling and it was chilly. The teacher told Haley to get his coat on or he would freeze to death. Haley went and got his coat. Then he went out into the school yard. It was a school yard much like other school yards, or I suppose so as I have not seen other school yards yet. Even if I had I would say it was much like other school yards as I have just discovered the expression 'much like' and I like it.

'Hello, Haley,' said Andersen.

Andersen was a huge Swede, standing well over five feet. He had blood on his chin where he had tried to shave himself. His shoulders were much like big shoulders.

'Hello, Andersen.'

'I am going hunting in the woods. Are you coming?'

Haley knew what he meant. They were going to look for rabbits. They had never caught one yet and Haley was glad inside himself because they said that when you cornered a rabbit it was much like a mountain lion and tried to bite you, only lower down, about the knees.

When they were in the woods, Andersen stopped and shivered.

'It is a funny feeling, hunting rabbits. It is like the feeling of the thing between a man and a woman.'

'What is the thing between a man and a woman?'

'I am not sure. I thought you knew.'

'No, I do not know. But I thought you knew.'

'No.'

They went on a way further and they watched the leaves fall from the trees and hit the ground, which is the way of leaves when they fall off the trees. Haley shivered and said it was cold. Andersen said nothing. Haley said it again. Andersen said that it was not too cold to hunt rabbits. Haley said he did not mean he was trying to get out of hunting rabbits, he only thought it was cold and that was all he thought.

'Look!' said Andersen. 'A rabbit!'

'Where?' said Haley.

'Over there.'

'I cannot see it.'

'It has gone now. It does not matter. Perhaps it was not a rabbit at all. It is very cold.'

'Shall we go back to school now?' said Haley.

They went back to school and did some more lessons and then Haley went home but he did not tell his parents of what had happened.

DR EVIL

The first James Bond story (Ian Fleming, $14\frac{1}{2}$)

James Bond strode into the hallway of Dr Evil's house, wearing an immaculate school blazer which had been made for him by Jacob Schneider of Lucerne, which I think is in Switzerland, and asked the receptionist to tell Dr Evil that James Bond had come to see him.

'Dr Evil?' she said into the phone. 'There is a boy called Bond to see you.'

'Who is almost 17,' said James.

'Who is only 17,' she said. 'Yes, sir. Will you take the lift to the third floor?'

When Bond left the lift at the third floor he found himself face to face with Dr Evil, a squat, ugly, horrible little man who was uncannily like a certain schoolmaster.

'What can I do for you, Master Bond?' he said leering.

Bond felt in his pocket casually to check that his $2\frac{1}{2}$lb catapult, made of choice elm wood by a master craftsman in Bond Street, which is a very important street near Piccadilly, was loaded. He only used the very best conkers, imported from his aunt in Ireland, which was better than most aunts who only sent you book tokens.

'I think you know what I have come for,' he said coolly, no, icily. 'You have my replica authentic Japanese destroyer which fires real hara-kiri aeroplanes, which you confiscated for your own devilish ends. Sir.'

The face of Dr Evil went pale and he reached for his poison gun, but before he could pull it out Bond had pounced. At lightning speed he fastened the evil man in a half-Nelson, gave him a Chinese burn, did a quick knuckle-crusher and punched him in the nose. Dr Evil sank lifeless to the ground, only he wasn't really dead. Like a flash, Bond entered the nearest room. There, on the bed, was the most fantastic blonde, really smashing, with no clothes on at all, if you know what I mean, like in books. There, on the table was his authentic Japanese destroyer.

'Who are you?' she gasped huskily gazing at the handsome stranger.

'I am James Bond and I am $16\frac{3}{4}$,' he said in as low a voice as possible. 'I have just killed your friend Dr Evil, but he will live.'

He strode to the table and picked up the destroyer. Before he left the room he turned to the girl, well, woman, and said:

'You will get cold lying around with no clothes on, anyway it looks silly, whatever they say in books. I would get a dressing gown on if I were you.'

Moments later there came the distinctive sound of Bond's super three-speed-gear Raleigh as he pedalled away down the drive.

LORD ARTHUR WENTWORTH'S BLACKBOARD

Oscar Wilde's first play (age fifteen)

(The scene is a richly decorated room, hung with damask curtains, rich brocade and the finest tapestries, but if you cannot get this your mother's dresses would do. There is a pale scent of incense and also the furniture is sumptuous. It is the Fifth Form at St Topaz's School. A young man is seated at a desk, which is Arthur, who is the pupil. Standing by the gem-encrusted blackboard is a young man, which is Basil, who is the teacher. As the curtain rises, Arthur is lighting a slim, delicate cigarette.)

Basil: You know it is against the school rules to smoke, Arthur.

Arthur: What is the point of rules if we do not break them?

Basil: You have just made an epigram. Do you know the derivation of the word 'epigram'?

Arthur: Like most words in English, it comes from the classics. Without the help of the Romans and Greeks, Englishmen would be hard put to it to express their contempt for foreign languages.

Basil: I sometimes wonder who is giving this lesson – you or me. Now, where was I?

Arthur: You were trying to persuade me that a knowledge of Canadian wheat production will enrich my career as a poet and artist.

Basil: My dear boy, one does not have a *career* as a poet. Poetry is too important to work at. One must content one's self with devoting one's self to it.

Arthur: Exactly. I shall write a play and with the proceeds withdraw to an exquisite house where I shall dedicate my life to a poem.

Basil: It is a charming thought. What will your play be about?

Arthur: It will be about two wonderful young men sitting in a classroom talking about art, poetry and Canadian wheat production. One must show the public one has taste and also has done one's lessons.

Basil: And how will the play end?

Arthur: Suddenly, without any warning at all.

(CURTAIN)

November 1973

RODIN'S
HOT
BATH-WATER

3
COUNTRY PURSUITS

'Frankly, Cleo, I'm more hurt than angry.'

Libby Purves

HUNTIN' SHOOTIN' AND MISSIN'

'Sleet!' he cried. 'Lovely!' and hurtled down a tussocky bank like the Queen's Own Kami-kaze Landrovers. I'd last seen this young man shivering pathetically under two rain-drops and a puff of autumn wind on a Suffolk beach, demanding to go home. Here on his home Fens, he was eerily transformed. He had organized me into trousers, under-trousers, three jerseys, four gloves, a string vest, a khaki hat, balaclava, vast ill-fitting waders, a disgustin' old shootin' jacket, and many socks. He had delicately proffered the loan of 'thermo-insulated underwear'. He had loaded up the resulting bundle along with his dogs, his fellow-shots, his cartridge-belt and a leathery, bloodstained Thing for hanging dead birds off. And with a final geary roar, he now leaped the last bank and parked beside a dyke.

'Wildfowling, you never know if you're going to get much luck at all,' he said apolo-getically. 'If it would only *snow*, we could get up to fifty in an afternoon. Now, it might just be two.' On the whole, I didn't mind. While not subscribing to the school of thought which engages in battles of wit and aniseed balls with infuriated MFH's in the shires, I was not yet conditioned to creeping around the marshes in borrowed thermo-nuclear underwear, blasting innocent im-migrant ducks out of the sky. Not that I personally presented much of a threat; with overclad arms unable to rise above elbow-level, no gun, and my usefulness confined to

the charge of the second, elderly and rather crazed, labrador, Paul. While the men armed themselves to the teeth, Paul and I got acquainted. They're very reserved, gundogs, very dour and sober even when crazed. Not demonstrative, indoor, ordinary dogs; they don't wear collars in case they catch them on wire and drown; they wag their tails when it rains and sit quietly in puddles; they watch the sky.

Any sport which keeps big dogs so en-tranced, I thought confusedly under my camouflage-hat, can't be all bad; and decided for the duration of at least one article to renege from my usual pose of sentimental cat-lover, keeping a benevolent distance from Nature while treading on the odd beetle. I re-aligned myself, shakily, with the ghosts and descendants of those fine, untroubled squires who ate off their own old silver, sat on their ancient furniture, disci-plined their dogs, and shot and ate their game-birds with the divine right of owner-ship. 'Anyway, the wildfowl wouldn't be in this country at all now, if it wasn't for people like us keeping our land wild for them,' said our host, tranquilly, looking up his double-barrels at a pintail. Bang.

He missed it, and the rest veered away. A flight of wild swans swung past, smugly unalarmed. If you're on the right schedule, these days, you're laughing. The fowlers, united in shotgun wedding with the orni-thologists, have to know a scaup-duck from a Savi's Warbler through the sleetiest haze; they learn lists of forbidden birds along with the rest of their sporting arcana of punt-gunning, Shooting Rights on Seawalls, camouflage, and the laying of ratproof nesting-baskets. 'It's a matter of respecting what you shoot,' he said severely, and took permitted, licensed aim at a passing teal.

(I think it was a teal. *You* try making notes on all fours in the rushes, without moving or letting the ducks see your white page flutter, and with a whiffling old labrador hitched to your frozen, gloved, writing wrist. I *think* he said teal.)

Anyway, ethical musings apart, it's hard to strike up any very close relationship with a wild duck. There it is on the wall, made of plaster; or being kept in a symbolic attic by depressed Norwegian playwrights; or flying with its mates across the East Anglian sky and BANG! stone cold dead in the water, and the fowlers see no harm in warming their chilly hands under its wings.

On some estates they rear the little ducks like pheasants, and when the season comes they drive them quacking towards the guns; at least out on the Fens the snipers wait for nightfall, stand sentry with the condensation freezing in their boots, study the Effect of Tides on Flight-Lines, and know the distant call of every migrant. 'At a *driven* shoot,' said one, contemptuously, watching a late pheasant twitching its last against his rubbered thigh, 'I wouldn't have had to shoot that thing standing on one foot with the other in a dyke, and a dead duck and a cartridge-belt between my legs. I'd have been sat on my bum on a shooting-stick, waiting for it to rise in front of me.'

And we tramped off, up to our knees in miniature ice-floes, through the weird marsh sunset. The farther guns reverberated oddly around the horizon, and the swans barked very far away, towards the sea. Hereward the Wake escaped his pursuers along these muddy paths, when the Fens were undrained, navigable in tiny coracles by shaggy Fenmen. *A grut black dog haunts this Fen,*

nigh as big as a calf, 'is eyes glowering red as blood an' big as bike-lamps ... Vague memories stirred of the seventh century, good St Guthlac assaulted by the wild amphibious race, *Great heads, lean faces, pale countenances, rugged thighs, broad lips, pre-*

posterous feet, open mouths, and hoarse cries ... They grew *woad* here till the war, they had a woad-mill ...

Rugged thighs. Preposterous feet. Every sucking, muddy step dragged the heel of my enormous waders away from the swaddled,

OUR SPORTING WICKETS

Fond Wife. 'HAROLD, DEAR, HAVE YOU TAKEN YOUR TEETH OUT?'

thermo-insulated foot, and they buckled and deformed in the rushes fit to alarm St Guthlac and all comers. Mercifully, we found our new pitch and stopped. The moon and two stars glimmered off the frozen reeds and they gave me a job to do: I had to raise a small tin object to my frozen lips and blow artistic widgeon-calls to attract them over us in the gloom. It looked like something stolen off an old-fashioned whistling kettle, and with it I apparently struck the exact widgeon equivalent of a raspberry. Only the aged dog responded, briefly. 'You'd better stop,' said John kindly after a while, 'or they'll begin to suspect something. GRAAAWWWNK?' – unaided – 'GRAWNNNKKK??'. Wings would whistle suddenly out of nowhere, and vanish. 'Is that a bird or a liver spot?' he muttered, shooting at it with a yellow, splintering flash. 'Liver spot.' 'Le mallard imaginaire,' I attempted, and did another, surprisingly seductive, duck-whistle. Unexpectedly, the junior dog appeared with a wet widgeon in his jaws, and presented it soberly to his master. The other hound was still attached to me, up to his knees in water and looking pensively at the moon; but something barked, deeply, and glowered in the distance like red bike-lamps. Unseen, preposterous feet made the reed-beds quake and shudder. The snow began to blow horizontally and settle on the unmoving fowlers.

But I think it was a certain heart-breaking shiver in my widgeon-calls that eventually drove the quarry away and us back to the Landrover. That, and the fact that someone had left the hipflask on the front seat. So we left Hereward, Guthlac, and the grut black dog to puzzle over the spoor of distorted size eleven waderprints and dragged labrador-feet, and took home our dead, wet, feathery booty. Six birds there were. Up in the howling black sky, six thousand more were laughing like so many whistling kettles.

January 1976

Michael Parkinson

JUST NOT CRICKET

As I was trying to point out to my oldest boy the other day, the proper cricketing heroes of my youth didn't go to the wicket encased in thigh pads, elbow protectors, chest armour and a crash helmet. Garfield Sobers took 'em off his chin and wearing no more than the hair on his head. Brian Close blocked bouncers with his bare chest and later in the dressing-room found a bruise with the ball maker's name on it, and the great and good Keith Miller once went straight from a night club to a cricket match and, wearing shiny black dancing pumps, led his Australian team into battle.

Like most things I tell my children it made not the slightest difference. The big one went off carrying his armour to play the first team and when I went down to see them later both sides were replicas of their professional brothers, from the tip of their metal-encased heads to their sweat-banded wrists (selling sweat-bands to English cricketers must be one of the cleverest merchandising ploys of all time).

The fact is that all British sport is now part of the same marketing exercise. The television camera points its eye and the agents, that new army of wheeler-dealers, shove their clients in front of it with as much of his person as is practical and decent tattooed with symbols and gimmicks. At present the brains of the industry are working on a scheme to incorporate advertising of one form or another on snooker players' backsides. Apart from being much appreciated by certain members of the viewing audience – or so research tells us – the aforesaid backsides have what is known in the business as a 'high visibility factor'. The trick is to exploit them without getting the owner arrested.

Anyhow, that's as maybe. The general point to be made is that as we become more saturated by these images of the new sporting gimmickry, the more we copy the styles and attitudes of our professional sportsmen, the more we are in danger of forgetting one of the most important of all sporting principles: that while *they* have to do it for money, *we* can afford to do it for fun.

Joe Mercer once observed (and we must never tire of quoting the classics) that the trouble with modern sport is that you rarely see anyone smile on the field of play. At the time he was talking about professional sport but today his observation would be equally pertinent about any level of any game.

My retirement from cricket as a player was hastened by one moment in my last season when, having been bowled by an absolute peach of a ball (pitching leg, hitting off – that's my story), I said to the bowler by way of a compliment, 'That would have bowled a century maker.' He replied with a snarl, '*You* wouldn't make a bloody century against me.'

I told this story once to the late Jack Fingleton who, in his latter days, was a disappointed observer of the decline of attitudes, both on and off a cricket field. I think what finally polished Jack off was the news that the England team to visit Australia contained a cricketer wearing an earring. Aluminium bats, purple sweaters, white balls and black sightscreens had already weakened Jack's will to live, but a cricketer wearing jewellery finally persuaded him to give up altogether.

Anyhow, after telling Jack about my run-in with the quick bowler, he reminded me that psychological warfare had always been a part of cricket, but what had changed over the years was the manner of delivery. The silken, humorous insult had been replaced by vulgar abuse. The Australians, who have a way with words, called it 'sledging'.

As an example of how it used to be, Jack told the story of making his debut for his club in Sydney and walking to the wicket with C. G. Macartney, the legendary Australian test cricketer. The young Fingleton trotted alongside the master as he strode to the wicket, eager to get everything right, to impress on his debut. Their walk to the middle was made in silence until as they approached the wicket, Macartney said to his partner, 'Remember, young man, watch out for the first ball.'

Jack wondered what the message might mean and decided that Macartney was telling him to be on his toes for the quick single. As Macartney settled down to face the first ball, the young Fingleton was trembling with eagerness and excitement. The fast bowler thundered in and as he approached the wicket so Macartney began a leisurely stroll down the wicket towards him. Jack was also backing up so the overall picture must have been of three people moving towards each other on a narrow pavement.

As the bowler bowled, Macartney, continuing his stroll, straight drove the ball back at head height causing Jack, the bowler and the umpire to fling themselves to the ground. The ball hit the sightscreen with a terrible crack and rebounded fifty yards onto the field.

Jack said that as he, the umpire and the bowler untangled themselves from the heap he was aware of Macartney standing next to him leaning nonchalantly on his bat. 'See what I mean about that first ball, young Fingleton? Always hit it back smack between their eyes. They don't much like it,' he said, smiling disarmingly at the bowler.

Mind you, not every aspect of style and wit has departed our cricket grounds. There are still exponents of the clever and subtle

THE BRITISH CHARACTER
LOVE OF OPEN-AIR SPORTS

put-down around – they just pop up in the most unexpected places. For instance, having retired from proper cricket and confined my playing to the odd appearance for a showbiz team, I was once standing in a dressing-room in Sheffield when a remarkable thing happened. I was naked at the time, having just showered, and alone in the room – my colleagues were at tea. Moreover, I had my back to the door. I heard it open, assumed it was my team mates returning and then a woman said, 'Excuse me, Mr Parkinson,' I turned round, trying to do impossibly difficult things with a handkerchief, to find myself in the company of an attractive young woman and her daughter. The woman appeared completely unfazed and her daughter simply sucked her thumb and stared at the strange embarrassed man in front of her. 'Sorry to bother you,' the woman said, 'but could I have your autograph?' I nodded my head. She advanced with an autograph book and as I invented

new contortions to take the book while holding on to the handkerchief, she asked, 'Do you have a pen?'

Now I have asked some daft questions in my time, but none as dumb as that. I indicated a coat where she might find a pen and then performed like a Bendy Toy while holding the book, pen, handkerchief, and writing my signature.

All this was observed with an unblinking stare by both mother and daughter, who seemed blissfully unaware of the bizarre picture we presented. I gave her the book. She thanked me and made to leave the pavilion. As she did she turned, smiled again and said, 'By the way, don't worry, I won't let on.'

It might be true, as Mr Mercer said, that no one smiles on the field of play anymore. But it's nice to know that the spectators still find plenty to laugh at.

May 1984

Frank Keating

AND THE EGG RAN AWAY WITH THE SPOON

I went to a school summer sports day last week, and a trampoline exhibition broke out. There wasn't even an egg-and-spoon for the Under-fives. Too competitive, you see. If they had put on a three-legged race, even the two Davids might have won a prize. But no competition, no first, second, third, and definitely no Booby.

And after Trampolinex, came the Mixed Maypole Dancing. Not a winner in sight. Before tea – all uniform rock buns, so no aggressive sporty type could be first in the queue to polish off the best jam sponge – we had Throwing the Cricket Ball. But nobody measured the distances; no marks even for artistic impression. They are dreary days on Britain's school sportsfields. Lots of Pansy Potters, and no little Victor Ludorums.

No more for the sake of a ribboned coat, or the selfish hope of a season's fame . . .

> *There's a breathless hush in the Close tonight,*
> *Ten to make and the match to win . . .*

Not any more there ain't.

Radical educationalists see sporting competition as a social evil. The modern view is that Muggins shouldn't excel at the crease, if Diddums is having to spend all day fetching the ball for him from deep square-leg. As Stuart Biddle, the secretary of the British Society of Sports Psychologists, put it last year:

> For many children, established school sports are sheer purgatory. Remember,

only about five per cent ever make the school team. Now team games and competitive events might serve a valuable purpose for those who excel, but the modern view is that sport is most beneficial when everyone can participate at their own level – and today tens of thousands of British children are participating in activities that once would have been considered 'exotica'.

Like sailing and mountaineering – and trampolining and mixed maypole dancing, I suppose.

Many of these 'activities' are not even on the school curriculum. They are voluntary and 'coached' outside school hours – the more so since the teachers' dispute ran (ironically) and ran. Though the good, earnest, misguided folk who plan policy for the Inner London Education Authority have their reasons – always passionately and cogently argued – fact is that the world as we know it in these matters may never be the same again. Apart from the odd bit of trampolining, probably the only organised team games the majority of this year's state school-leavers will play will be Monopoly, or those inside pin-table frames. A comprehensive, you might say, disaster. Oh, my Gatting and my Botham long ago . . .

Soccer, because it really is the people's game and for the ease with which just a handful of guys can throw down a couple of goalpost-coats, should manage to survive among the Yumpies – that is, the Young Unfit Municipal Park Players. But both codes of rugby (though the League clubs are fashioning a healthy enough Saturday morning out-of-school yahoo) and cricket, especially, could be deprived totally of their whole and wholesome plebeian intake within a generation – and the heritage of these two great national games would revert to the public schoolboys of last century. That would be a tragedy.

To be sure, it is a good bet that Mike

Gatting will not only be the first, but also the last comprehensive schoolboy to be England's cricket captain. He was at John Kelly's Boys, whence he graduated to Brondesbury CC, after answering an ad for coaching sessions in the *Willesden & Brent Chronicle*. Meanwhile, of course, Ian Botham had been the first sec.mod. skipper of England (having gone to Bucklers' Mead in Yeovil after deliberately failing his 11-plus, he says, because they didn't play soccer at the local grammar school); and Keith Fletcher was the first village school former pupil to toss for England (Comberton, in Cambridgeshire, which was too small even to have a cricket team).

These three, hitherto class barriered, social advances in English cricket happened only in the last half dozen years. A breakthrough no sooner achieved than thrown away, it seems.

It is odd, don't you think, how the competitive ethic in sport has become so unfashionable in Mrs Thatcher's macho reign. But it was easy: the PE teachers of ILEA simply dispensed with any judges or 'tribunals' – for any pastime, even trampolining and mixed maypole dancing, can become a ruthless competitive sport if played and judged on a strict set of codified rules. Why, even the waterlogged and breathless synchronised swimming of Tracey and Debra left off being

GOING TO COVER
Brown (who has given Tomkins, from Town, a Mount). 'YOU NEEDN'T BE THE LEAST AFRAID. IT'S ONLY HIS PLAY. HE'LL BE ALL RIGHT AFTER HE HAS BEEN OVER A FEW FENCES!'

a recreation and became a narrow-eyed Olympic sport, once some ruddy twit decorated it with a set of regulations. Plus, of course, a team of po-faced judges, wearing gold-buttoned blazers, and marching about, poolside, with clipboards.

The Victorian values of Dr Arnold's missionary Muscular Christians in Dickens's inner city had it that if you saw a group of street urchins throwing rocks at random, you did not call the Peelers and have them locked up – but went out and organised the rules for a rock-throwing contest. And everyone was happy. And thus the Modern Olympiad.

There are new rules now. Or, rather, none. *Decline and Fall* is the sum of it – as even the most unathletic Mr Waugh so gloriously chronicled in his first great novel. Hear ye this, for olde tyme's sake:

'The course,' said Paul, 'starts at the pavilion, goes round that clump of elms...'

'Beeches,' corrected Lady Circumference, loudly.

'... and ends in front of the bandstand. Starter, Mr Prendergast; timekeeper, Captain Grimes.'

'I shall say, "Are you ready? one, two, three!" and then fire,' said Mr Prendergast. 'Are you ready? One' – there was a terrific report. 'Oh dear! I'm sorry' – but the race had begun.

Clearly Tangent was not going to win; he was sitting on the grass crying because he had been wounded in the foot by Mr Prendergast's bullet. Philbrick carried him, wailing dismally, into the refreshment tent, where Dingy helped him off with his shoe. His heel was slightly grazed. Dingy gave him a large slice of cake, and he hobbled out surrounded by a sympathetic crowd.

'That won't hurt,' said Lady Circumference, 'but I think someone ought to remove the pistol from that old man

before he does anything serious!'

Happy days at the school sports. When childhood summers were bathed in sunlight; when winners swanked, and losers blubbed. Now all together please, folks, let's hear it for the final formation of the mixed maypole dance...

June 1987

Kenneth Allsop

WILL YOU RIDE IT HOME OR EAT IT HERE?

Coming as it did just after the Lord Chancellor's heart-lifting Margate message to Young Conservatives of the urgent 'need to be tougher' about such manifestations of global rottenness as strikers, go-slowers, sit-inners, muggers, permissives, the Angry Brigade, the Black September gang and the Welsh Language Society, the case of the Westmorland fox dramatically underlined his point.

While my veins were throbbing tumescently with new manly corpuscles from Lord Hailsham's 'organ note of patriotism', I noticed the disturbing report about this skunk of a fox near John Peel's old galloping ground which has thrice lured hounds of the Lunedale Hunt to disaster under the wheels of M6 traffic and over a quarry edge – before cunningly doubling away unscathed.

'That fox needs shooting,' Huntsman John Nicholson sombrely told the press, and I should think so too. When the subversive impertinence which is corroding our wholesome standards into mouldy old dough spreads from student rabble and trade unionist wreckers, and infects even our furred aborigines, the time indeed has come to be tougher. If that bolshie fox is so unsporting that it won't let itself be killed according to the rules of the game, then blasted with shot it must be. Doesn't it know that it isn't cricket? Myself, I'd rather see it publicly hanged, after a healthy spell exhibited in a municipal compound and pelted with garbage by the jeering populace, on the lines recommended by another crusader for law and order, the Tory MP for Luton, Mr Charles Simeons.

Although Lord Hailsham enumerated every single blight gnawing away at the corsets which kept Britannia that upright figure, with prongs poised like the park-keeper of a rubbishy world, he didn't actually mention non-human subversives. When he brought in the Icelandic trawler troubles he didn't blame the cod. But he is a man who likes to see the fencing kept stout – and possibly reinforced with some spiked iron railings – to hold everything in its proper place, legally, constitutionally and traditionally. Similarly, while Mr Nicholson is understandably fed up with his valuable though obviously not overbright dogs being monotonously tricked into hurling themselves under container trucks and over precipices, there does seem to be a perceptible sharing of outlook. Like an art school dropout turned urban guerilla, or those arty chappies coming out with things like *Last Tango in Brooklyn*, that fox is upsettingly deviating from its allotted harmless and supervised role. And if there's one thing we British won't put up with, it's disruption of our convenient and comfortable schizophrenia about animals.

We chase them and praise them, we cook them and coddle them, we stuff them and stroke them, we breed them and exterminate them, we legislate for a wild bird's right to freedom and we lawfully run concentration camps for broiler fowls. Ladies who cred-

itably campaigned against catching rabbits in steel-fanged gins keep tabbies whose bellies are sleekly round with song thrushes. Gentlemen who enjoy the testing rigours of putting bullets into deer (hopefully in a fatal place so that they don't dawdle to their death with a gangrenous limb) slam bull-fighting as a barbarous wop entertainment. People distressed by vivisection don't mind whether rats die of strychnine or in spring traps. Favoured girls cuddle their chihuahuas against their leopard skin coats. Kindly dog-lovers in tweeds derive quiet pleasure from persuading trout to drive barbed steel hooks through their jaws.

Doubtless there are many vegetarian conservationists, but personally I don't know one ornithologist who won't return from an exhilarating estuary-outing making census counts of migrating wildfowl and satisfy his whetted appetite on roast pheasant or jugged hare. I don't smugly exclude myself. As a lifelong bird-watcher, so would I – although, with weird avoidance of logic, I would primly turn down plovers' eggs on the menu or that Cypriot delicacy of bottled swallows and warblers.

We never tire of declaiming that we are a nation of animal-lovers. Curiously, we apparently require the surveillance of such police forces as the League Against Cruel Sports, the Royal Society for the Protection of Birds, the Performing Animals' Defence League, and, for 150 years, the Royal Society for the Prevention of Cruelty to Animals.

Not that this most venerable and respectable of institutions is exactly single-minded in its objectives. It has for long been lambasted for its toleration of hunting and its benign smile upon the little rural ritual of 'blooding' children, especially Royal apprentices. Despite its indisputably majestic record of good works (it brings 300 successful prosecutions yearly and has weighty influence in establishment circles) some critics think it could use its equally majestic

£5 million assets to finance more energetic clean-ups. It is currently under attack from militants who consider it tepidly inert about the more barbaric blood sports and the more callous factory farming; furthermore, this month a petition signed by 15,000 reformers goes to the Society's patron, the Queen herself, demanding keener concern from the RSPCA for domestic animals.

In a way, the RSPCA symbolises our overall ambivalence and compromise about the lesser breeds. Providing they don't make themselves a nuisance, or compete for space and food, we will lazily – and under regulation – show a fickle paternalistic solicitude to certain favoured brutes, as long as they submit to being exploited, tamed and slaughtered.

In middle class tribal customs the horse (as Lt Mark Phillips might vouch) frequently predominates in emotional attachment. And yet, while there is clearly no call for a Battersea Nags' Home, this same kingdom of devotees of four-legged pals leaves the RSPCA to deal with (ie, destroy) 350,000 abandoned dogs and cats annually.

What it comes down to is that our compassion is flexible as a glitterwax plaything. Our fondest feelings are reserved for creatures which resemble us – so they must be all right, eh, gang? There are exceptions. The toad and the hippo are acceptable because they're 'comical', and, while Beatrix Potter and A. A. Milne dived straight for the sentimental jugular with Flopsy Bunny and Winnie-the-Pooh, even the fierce and the slimy and the smelly have been safely sanitised and anthropomorphised in comics (viz, Tiger Tim) and now TV (viz, Basil Brush and Brian the Snail). But the ones we really take a shine to are reassuringly familiar in their winningly cute way.

It's no coincidence that zoologists have statistically found that among the top-of-the-pops are the chimp, the bush-baby and the panda. All have flat cherubic faces, frontal eyes, hair rather than scales and erect postures: mimic human beings, just like some of our best friends or our own kiddie-winkies.

We modified the dog. By Frankenstein tinkering we kneaded into existence contrived cupcake visages, and of course taught them to sit up and beg, thus imitating our stance. Among birds, the penguin – that aldermanic waddler – is high in the charts, along with the owl (likewise of upright build and round-eyed and chubby-looking, concealing its assassin's nature beneath a Billy Bunter guise). It follows that penguin and owl are the most popular humanoid bird-dolls in the toy shops.

My theory has always been that the nub of the notorious *Oz* Schoolkids' Issue case was instinctual but unarticulated outrage at the lewd Rupert the Bear cartoon: the caricature caricatured, the innocent nursery manikin distorted by a dastardly pen into a rampantly horny rapist. The bubble was, you might say, pricked, and empires have caved in from less cruel apostasy. Is nothing sacred – not even teddy-bears?

Even when we don't shrink them into poppets and puppets, we have at least to pretend that we respect our less advanced companions on the planet. For all that he might furtively smack his lips over every last drop of gravy, I doubt that Humphrey Lyttelton would risk animal-fans' wrath by including in his food guide some Beauchamp Place hashery reviving peacocks' brains, nightingales' tongues and casseroled Pekinese.

We vaguely enjoy seeing those fluffy lambs and dappled cattle in the meadows, an aesthetic element of the pastoral scene, yet as soon as the electric stunner has been applied and the throat knifed, we without inner stress mentally convert them into carcasses. Can't be helped, can it? They get the chop, we get our chops. Consciences assuaged, we crunch up every meaty particle. Yet, although we eccentrically draw a limit at the sheep's eyes which Bedouins munch, we eat the rest – from sheep's brains down to pigs' trotters, not neglecting the tongue, heart, kidneys and testicles in between. And in a Greek restaurant we probably go yum-yum over *kokkoretsi*, which is the entire insides of a sheep, not omitting lungs and stomach, with the bowels grilled around skewers like grisly maypoles.

I wouldn't say that we are cynically hypocritical in our attitudes toward brute creation. Plutarch argued that much of life's cruelty stemmed from man's lust for meat. Nevertheless we won through because about three million years ago we learned to bring down the mammoth and suck its drumsticks, and I think that nowadays we do (just a mite) more sensitively care about our dumb friends' welfare and survival. Someone like Baden-Powell really would seem bafflingly out of joint today: that avid pig-sticker who rhapsodised about the 'manly and tip-top' sport which provided an ecstatic 'taste of the brutal' – and proceeded to found the Boy Scouts, pledged to be kind to animals.

We've been educated that it's pleasanter to phase out the concrete jungle zoo where animals are gawped at through iron bars, and now have so many safari parks that the unwary bluebell-picker can't be sure that he won't trip over a lion in that roadside ash copse. At the same time we prefer to keep off our holiday itinerary the pre-fab Auschwitzes which mass-produce our cheap poultry and supermarket meat. Most of us would no longer lock a robin in a cage – quite apart from whether it would put all heaven in a rage – but we don't really care if a chicken goes insane, cooped in windowless batteries, debeaked and dosed with tranquillisers and antibiotics, if the price is right.

April 1973

Honest Stan Reynolds

IF THEY ASKED ME, I COULD MAKE A BOOK

Despite much unselfish work on my part, the bookies have been complaining of making some losses lately. They threw out some astronomical figures about their losses at the Grand National. Here, of course, is the biggest mug's game in the world and betting on the National is the mug de la mug. Year after year you can hear them laughing and singing as they stuff the suckers' money into the pockets of their overly loud checked suits.

I went to the National this year with my friend Cedric and his son Eric. Eric had never been to a racecourse before. Cedric went up to a bookie, made his own bet and then made a bet for Eric on the same horse. Eric wanted to have his own marker so if the horse won he could go to the bookie and collect and all that.

'What!!!' screamed the bookmaker. All around us people are pressing forward, eagerly waving bank notes, trying to force their money into the bookie's hands. But he stands there, glaring down from his little box at Cedric.

'What,' he says, 'you want two markers?'

'It's for Eric,' Cedric explained.

Smilin' Jack, the Punter's Pal, glares at the teenaged Eric and then snaps, 'These ... markers ...' The dots are to show how slow he is saying this. And you must remember there is all this time this great crush of bodies all around us, all waving fistsful of folding money trying to place a bet with Smilin'

Jack. The crush is very much like Cartier Bresson's famous photograph of the rush on the Shanghai bank; at least this is what I thought of at the time.

'These ... markers ... cost, a PENNY!!! apiece,' Smilin' Jack, the Punter's Pal, bellows out above the heads of all the eager suckers.

What a lesson that was. What a gaze into the heart of the bookmaker. The *black* heart of the black hearted cursed bookmaker. The name of the lesson is THRIFT. Not penny-wise and pound foolish. The lesson is take care of the pennies and the pounds will take care of themselves.

Bookies are the worst sort of penny pinching swine you will meet in a long day's march to the North or the South. And what's perhaps even worse, they laugh at the suckers. A fellow I know named Captain Mac, who apparently acquired a taste for hob-nobbing with low life when he was a kid in New Brunswick and used to rack 'em down at the pool hall, told me that a bookmaker friend of his has just retired and built himself a joint in the Bahamas somewhere and he calls his house The Doubles in honour of all the suckers who thought they could bet doubles and win.

When I saw the first four favourites coming in one, two, three, four at the National, even though I had no money on them, a little song sang in my heart thinking of the bookies paying money out.

The Tote, of course, allows you to escape from actual contact with the bookie. Efficient, old time schoolmarmy, motherly type women sit behind a grilled window, just like in a bank or on visiting day up at the state pen, and you pass your worn florins or tinny new pence to them. But you need a degree from M.I.T. really to get in there and bet on the Tote in any serious manner. Or put it another way: How come those yobboes who can bet on the Tote with effortless ease, making all manner of complicated bets, how come those yobboes are still yobboes? Why don't they have degrees from M.I.T.?

(At the Derby one year with my pals Billy and Dave, Arnold and Alf, the gypsies came swarming down upon us shouting, 'Hey Gorgio, wanna buy a hot tip?' They press tiny, sealed envelopes into your hands, whispering that you're not to open them until just before the race – like sealed orders on the high seas. If you don't buy they give you the black spot. After we bought, Alf said, 'If they know so much, how come they still got to be gypsies?' It was a good question.)

Most of the time, like every one else, I never lay eyes on the gee gees, but, now that they are naming races after baked beans, Ascot and the rest of the courses seem anyway to have lost a bit of their dignity. I go to betting shops, slinking in like a high school kid going in to Spotted Mary's back in Cody, Wyoming.

'Hi, Gus,' I usually say to Gus, who is sitting behind the mesh biting his finger-nails, fretting himself to death about whether seven rooms will be enough in the villa he is building in Benidorm. 'How's the new caps on the daughter's teeth?'

I take a personal interest in Gus. I'm paying part of his son's Borstal fees. And the other day his youngest daughter almost ran over me in a trick car which I and some other suckers went shares in buying. You get some idea of the mysterious way in which God works when you take a look at bookies' kids.

A little while ago I always also had a cheery greeting for the curvy blonde in the shop, a girl who looked like she ought to be called Trixie or Dolores but was only Linda. A month or so ago Mrs Gus got wise. Now Mrs Gus, a hatchet-faced woman who used to be something big in the Cheka before she met Gus, sits there knitting like Madame Defarge. Every now and then she gives Gus a dirty look and he coughs nervously into the back of his hand.

Dave – of Billy and Dave, Arnold and Alf –

rang me the other weekend from Plymouth where he is working building the new docks. Dave had a hot tip for the Ascot 2,000 Guineas. He got it from some jockeys and trainers he is working with. It was only after these fancies failed to materialise at anything faintly resembling the winning post that I began to wonder what sort of jockeys and trainers would be working building the new docks at Plymouth; where Dave's horses were running the finish was merely a rumour. But the point of this is just how distrustful, how unsporting your average bookie is.

'Say, Gus,' I say, 'what odds will you give me on Cambridge?' I had just remembered they were running the Oxford–Cambridge boat race that afternoon, with Oxford favoured. Gus gives me a very suspicious look, a look like his wife usually gives him. I coughed nervously into the back of my hand.

'*You realise our 100 to 1 against your horse is nothing **personal**, sir?*'

Gus knows I am an American and suddenly I can see that he thinks that maybe I have been setting him up all these years for this big number, the great boat race fix. I can see that Gus is thinking I am a member of the Mafia. If Gus were an American, he'd be a member of the Mafia. There are two Harvard men in the Oxford boat. Maybe I got their old grandmothers tied up in a cellar somewhere.

'How much?' he said in the deep unsteady voice of a man who is about to throw his plantation and his daughter Lula Belle into the jack pot.

'Five bob,' I said, cold as ice.

Gus did some lightning calculations. 'The Cambridge boat's got a nine and a half stone advantage,' he said. 'And only twice in the history of the race has a boat with that advantage been beat and each time the winning boat was Cambridge.'

'Listen,' I said, 'you sure you don't want to check the wind conditions?'

'It's North West,' he said. 'It could very well be a sinking wind.'

'To hell with it,' I said, ringing the coins on the counter, 'I'll take Oxford.'

'I can't give you even money,' Gus said.

Infuriated I raised the stakes to 80p. Gus wrote me out a slip. I put it in my pocket and headed for the door. 'I'll be seeing you,' he said.

'Wanna bet?' I said. Against all the odds Cambridge won the boat race again. From now on I'm sticking to horses. I know horses don't bet on people but at least it's the sport of kings. But then, how many of *them* do you see knocking around these days?

August 1973

Old Lady (at Victoria Station). 'OH, PORTER, HAS THERE BEEN A RAILWAY ACCIDENT?'
Porter. 'ACCIDENT! NO, LADY. THEY'VE JUST COME BACK FROM ENJOYIN' THEIRSELVES AT THE WINTER SPORTS.'

William Makepeace Thackeray

THE SNOBS OF ENGLAND

By One of Themselves

ON SOME COUNTRY SNOBS

Something like a journal of the proceedings at the Evergreens may be interesting to those foreign readers of *Punch*, who, as CONINGSBY says, want to know the customs of an English gentleman's family and household. There's plenty of time to keep the Journal. Piano strumming begins at six o'clock in the morning; it lasts till breakfast, with but a minute's intermission, when the instrument changes hands, and MISS EMILY practises in place of her sister, MISS MARIA.

In fact, the confounded instrument never stops: when the young ladies are at their lessons, MISS WIRT hammers away at those stunning variations, and keeps her magnificent fingers in exercise.

I asked this great creature in what other branches of education she instructed her

pupils? 'The modern languages,' says she modestly. 'French, German, Spanish, and Italian, Latin and the rudiments of Greek if desired. English of course; the practice of Elocution, Geography and Astronomy, and the Use of the Globes, Algebra, (but only as far as quadratic equations); for a poor ignorant female, you know, MR SNOB, cannot be expected to know everything. Ancient and Modern History no young woman can be without; and of these I make my beloved pupils *perfect mistresses*. Botany, Geology, and Mineralogy, I consider as amusements. And with these I assure you we manage to pass the days at the Evergreens not unpleasantly.'

Only these, thought I – what an education! But I looked in one of MISS PONTO's manuscript song books and found five faults of French in four words; and in a waggish mood asking MISS WIRT whether DANTE ALGIERY was so called because he was born at Algiers? received a smiling answer in the affirmative, which made me rather doubt about the accuracy of MISS WIRT's knowledge.

When the above little morning occupations are concluded, these unfortunate young women perform what they call Callisthenic Exercises in the garden. I saw them to-day, without any crenoline, pulling the garden roller.

Dear MRS PONTO was in the garden too, and as limp as her daughters; in a faded bandeau of hair, in a battered bonnet, in a holland pinafore, in pattens, on a broken chair, snipping leaves off a vine. MRS PONTO measures many yards about in an evening. Ye heavens! what a guy she is in that skeleton morning costume!

Besides STRIPES, they keep a boy called THOMAS, or TUMMUS. TUMMUS works in the garden or about the pigstye and stable; THOMAS wears a page's costume of eruptive buttons, as thus:–

When anybody calls, and STRIPES is out of the way, TUMMUS flings himself like mad into THOMAS's clothes, and comes out metamorphosed like Harlequin in the pantomime. To-day, as MRS P was cutting the grape-vine, as the young ladies were at the roller, down comes TUMMUS like a roaring whirlwind, with 'Missus, Missus! there's coompany coomin!' Away skurry the young ladies from the roller, down comes MRS P. from the old chair, off flies TUMMUS to change his clothes, and in an incredibly short space of time SIR JOHN HAWBUCK, my LADY HAWBUCK, and MASTER HUGH HAWBUCK are introduced into the garden with brazen effrontery by THOMAS, who says 'Please SIR JAN and my Lady to walk this year way: *I know* Missus is in the rosegarden.'

And there, sure enough, she was!

In a pretty little garden bonnet, with beautiful curling ringlets, with the smartest of aprons and the freshest of pearl-coloured gloves, this amazing woman was in the arms of her dearest LADY HAWBUCK. 'Dearest LADY HAWBUCK, how good of you! Always among my flowers! can't live away from them!'

'Sweets to the sweet! hum – aha–haw!' says SIR JOHN HAWBUCK, who piques himself on his gallantry, and says nothing without 'a-hum – a-ha – a-haw!'

'Whereth yaw pinnafaw?' cries MASTER HUGH, '*We* thaw you in it, over the wall, didn't we, Pa?'

'Hum – a-ha – a-haw!' burst out SIR JOHN, dreadfully alarmed, 'Where's PONTO? Why wasn't he at Quarter Sessions? How are his birds this year, MRS PONTO – have those Carabas pheasants done any harm to your wheat? a-hum – a-ha – a-haw!' and all this while he was making the most ferocious and desperate signals to his youthful heir.

'Well, she *wath* in her pinnafaw, wathn't she Ma?' says HUGH, quite unabashed; which question LADY HAWBUCK turned away with a sudden query regarding the dear, darling daughters, and the *enfant terrible* was removed by his father.

'I hope you weren't disturbed by the music,' PONTO says. 'My girls, you know, practise four hours a-day, you know – must do it, you know – absolutely necessary. As for me, you know I'm an early man, and in my farm every morning at five – no, no laziness for *me*.'

The facts are these. PONTO goes to sleep directly after dinner on entering the drawing-room, and wakes up when the ladies leave off practice at ten. From seven till ten, and from ten till five, is a very fair allowance of slumber for a man who says he's *not* a lazy man. It is my private opinion, that when PONTO retires to what is called his 'study', he sleeps too. He locks himself up there daily two hours with the newspaper.

I saw the *Hawbuck* scene out of the Study

which commands the garden. It's a curious object, that Study. PONTO's library mostly consists of boots. He and STRIPES have important interviews here of mornings, when the potatoes are discussed, or the fate of the calf ordained, or sentence passed on the pig, &c. All the major's bills are docketed on the Study table and displayed like a lawyer's briefs. Here, too, lie displayed his hooks, knives, and other gardening irons, his whistles, and strings of spare buttons. He has a drawer of endless brown paper for parcels, and another containing a prodigious and never-failing supply of string. What a man can want with so many gig-whips I can never conceive. These, and fishing-rods, and landing-nets, and spurs, and boot-trees, and balls for horses and surgical implements for the same, and favourite pots of shiny blacking, with which he paints his own shoes in the most elegant manner, and buck-skin gloves stretched out on their trees, and his gorget, sash, and sabre of the Horse Marines, with his boot-hooks underneath in a trophy; and the family medicine-chest, and in a corner the very rod with which he used to

A NICE GAME FOR TWO OR MORE

'—— FIXING HER EYES ON HIS, AND PLACING HER PRETTY LITTLE FOOT ON THE BALL, SHE SAID, "NOW, THEN, I AM GOING TO CROQUET YOU!"
AND CROQUET'D HE WAS COMPLETELY.' (*From Rose to Emily*)

whip his son, WELLESLEY PONTO, when a boy (WELLESLEY never entered the 'study' but for that awful purpose) – all these, with *Mogg's Road Book*, the *Gardener's Chronicle*, and a backgammon board, form the MAJOR's library. Under the trophy there's a picture of MRS PONTO, in a light-blue dress and train, and no waist, when she was first married; a fox's brush lies over the frame, and serves to keep the dust off that work of art.

'My library's small,' says PONTO, with the most amazing inducement, 'but well selected, my boy – well selected. I have been reading the *History of England* all the morning.'

October 1846

Alan Coren

THE COMPLEAT BUNGLER

to the Right Worshipful
DR RICHARD GORDON
of Dunpractisin,
in the Parish of Bromley,
my most honoured friend

Sir, I have made so ill use of your former favours, as by them to be encouraged to entreat, that they may be enlarged to the *patronage* and *protection* of this disquisition: and I have a modest confidence that I shall not be denied, because it is a discourse of *fish* and *fishing*, of which you are so great a master.

Further, indeed, so great a teacher: having, in the brief space of a single *East Grinstead* day, so effortlessly inducted me into the mistery as to persuade me to the assurance that I may now set down the substance of all that I have learned, for the *instruction* and *delight* of any human soul wishing to follow the example of,

SIR,
Your most affectionate friend,
And most humble servant,
A.C.

Chapter I

Conference betwixt an Angler and his Pupil in a Car-Park above the River, the Devices of their Craft having been removed from the Boot

PISCATOR. First, the rod.

PUPIL. I note, Master, that the bag contains three of them: the first frail and titchy, the second more substantial, and the third of some girth with a sturdy lozenge on the end. I take it that the first is for little fish, *exempli gratia*, Tadpole, Scampus, Oyster, and the like; the second for such of their more mature neighbours as Lobster, Pilchard, Kipper, *et cetera*; and the stoutest for the swift despatch of – *quid?* – Rock Salmon, perhaps, or Tuna? Even, perchaunce, the Large Fillet?

PISCATOR. No, Sir, they are but one rod, cunningly fashioned for portability's sake into three sections, which one assembles by firmly pushing each into its senior sibling. Do it thus.

PUPIL. 'Tis done! Egad, how the fellow swishes! See how the topmost bit flies, twenty yards or more, true as a dart, into yonder hatchback! Observe the depth of the gash, laying bare the rude red undercoat! Have I not done passing well? Why, were that not Signor Volvo but plain Johnny Haddock, that latter worthy would even now he floating belly up, Master, would he not, awaiting nought but the sizzling skillet and mayhap a chip or two to complete our rapture?

PISCATOR. I fear, Sir, you misprise the principle. Were you to have assembled the rod correctly, so as not to have engendered such repairs to coachwork which we may, with God's good grace, yet be fortunate enough to avoid underwriting by this expedient of hopping nimbly into the refugile trees on one wader, I should have been able to demonstrate to you the finesse of the true method by which the trout is lured to his foredestined doom.

PUPIL. Aha! A *trout*, eh? If I divine aright, one sprinkles a trout with almonds until he must perforce sink beneath their weight, upon which one simply flicks his inert corse from the water with the rod!

PISCATOR. Not exactly.

PUPIL. I have seen them with a pea pressed into the eye-socket, but it seems a cruel method for a sportsman.

PISCATOR. Remark, Sir, upon this little tin.

Chapter II

The Sportsmen arriving at their riparian Vantage, a lively Discourse ensues upon Bait

PUPIL. I have now noted the tin, Master. It is a receptacle for Old Pompey Shag. Curse me for a wittering fool, wool-gathered by pea and almond, I had clear forgot that the commonalty of brother trout is smoked! How do we go about it, Master? Depth-charge him with subterranean bubbles so that he surfaces, coughing, to be smote fin and gill with Colleague Rod? Release a perfumed and alluring cloud above the . . .

PISCATOR. I pray you, Sir, but open the tin.

PUPIL. Great Neptune! Tufts of Old Pompey, cunningly enbarbed – doubtless we waft these, smoking, across the dappled surface, the trout rises, as the phrase is, to the bait, intent upon a swift drag, and Ho!

PISCATOR. These, Sir, are flies.

PUPIL. Flies? And so tame?

PISCATOR. Their names are March-brown, Hairy Mary, Gnat, Butcher, Sedge –

PUPIL. Great Heavens, Master, are these not all from *Henry IV Part II*?

PISCATOR. – Yellow Mallard, Peter Ross, Green Chomper, Dunkeld, Welshman's Curse –

PUPIL. Stop! These are not flies, but pets! How may a man so stiffen his heart as to commit these enchristened souls, like ill-favoured Jonah, to the fish's belly?

PISCATOR. You do go on, Sir. These are but tufted feather, wedded to a hook. Follow my actions: take up the reel, secure it thus, thread through the line so, and affix the fly.

PUPIL. Which?

PISCATOR. Sniff the wind, note the cloud, observe the foliage, recall the month. The little brown bugger, I think.

PUPIL. Farewell, then, Little Brown Bugger!

PISCATOR. That is not necessary. Cast, so!

PUPIL. Aha! Forgive me, Master, for a fool! I had not realised that the technique called for no tearful parting taken of our tiny brethren. Not until I cast was it borne in upon me that the fly in fact remains in the tree, cleverly stuck fast by its trusty barb, and it is the reel that flies out across the water! Did I succeed in hitting a fish, Master?

Chapter III

The Pupil having waded into the Stream to retrieve his Reel, an earnest Enquiry is put by him upon his Return

PUPIL. I noted, Master, that others of our neighbour confraternity, when I was in midstream, began hurling stones. Some quite substantial. Do we not feel it to be a trifle inconsiderate, not to say dangerous, to continue so keenly to pelt fish when a gentleman brother of the angle – having fallen over and sunk as the result of his waders becoming filled with water upon his bending to grope for his reel – is thrashing about helplessly in the river? Do not, pray, reply that they perhaps did not see me, since lo! the froth of my recent hapless endeavours even now continues to mark the site of my misfortune.

PISCATOR. I was not, Sir, about so to reply. I wonder – now that you have so commendably grasped a deal of what is required of a man wishing to be left to fish alone, miles, perhaps, from the irritating distractions of his close acquaintances – whether the time has not come for us to separate ourselves one from another, the better to concentrate upon our sport?

PUPIL. Do you think so, Master?

PISCATOR. Yes.

Chapter IV

The Pupil, having been directed to a distant and unattended Stretch of Water and trudged thither, dangles from the long Twig – with which his thoughtful Master has so generously replaced the bothersome rod – the String to which his Master has so deftly attached the grey piece of Wonderloaf which the Pupil has been assured is the favourite Tid-bit of the Rainbow Trout.

PUPIL. The true, nay the sweetest, object of this peculiar exercise being, as I am given to understand it, not merely the sport itself – that transpiring to consist of little more than standing frozen in the drizzle and throwing coloured feathers into the murk on the remote chance of persuading a little bony item to so hook its lip as to afford oneself the pleasure of disengaging it, banging the glum head on a fencepost, and bearing the glau-

cous remains home in the fond hope of foisting them onto some luckless acquaintance prepared to eat them before they rot – but the random and discursive reflections which haply proceed from the benign solitude in which the activity is pursued, I must now address myself to this latter luxury.

Certainly, this present aqueous tract is more generative of observation than that other; which is beyond question why my Master chose it for me, today's object being my seduction to not only the nub and axle but also the spokes and outer rim of fishing. I see now that it is not a part of the main effluence at all, but a green pond so thickly coated that not only does my bread float upon the water, but that any trout rising to partake of it would be most like to stun itself upon the verdant ceiling of its habitation, thus sparing the novitiate the daunting and unsavoury task of braining it. I should be constrained to do no more than wade out and retrieve it with one of the many pots and pans with which this seminary spot is so thoughtfully girt, thus graduating Brother Trout from his breakfast to mine own in one fell swoop!

I note there is also a fine brass bedstead in it; and, floating beside, a choice of several bespoke mattresses, placed, I should be confident to hazard, so that the novice – as yet untrained to the patience and stamina of the vertically practised – may indulge that horizontal relief which calls across the slime to rheumy knee and aching vertebra.

Yet further: were, perchaunce, the gay Sussex sleet to lose a little of its appeal, the major part of a charming old Transit has been thoughtfully sited at the water's edge to afford snug rustic refuge from the pluvial caprice, so that the angler may sit as free from care as Virgil's Tityrus and his Melibeous did under their broad beech tree.

So, then, let me, as my gently sinking boots secure me ever more reassuringly into God's blessed property, offer thanks unto

'Did you know that the
most popular sport in
Britain is buying
equipment?'

'... And that's only the size of the fly.'

'That must be the smallest
man ever to catch a
salmon!'

my other and scarcely less venerated Master. *Ave, Doctor, flos doctorem!* I will not forget the doctrine which Socrates taught scholars, that they should not think to be honoured so much for being philosophers, as to honour philosophy by their virtuous lives. You advised me to the like concerning angling, and I shall endeavour to do so. This is my firm resolution; so when I would beget content, and increase confidence in the power, and wisdom, and providence of Almighty God, let me but place myself thus, as a conduit between the waters which are under the firmament and the waters which are above the firmament, my streaming eyes upon the bobbing lager can which toils not neither does it spin, my throbbing ear a host to God's wondrously fashioned gnat, my nostrils thickening with a salutary *memento mori* of man's brief tenancy, and in my frozen hand the inert symbol of hope's ludicrous vanity, and – thus sited four-square within that microcosm which may stand for all we are and all we may ever expect to be – I may, like every angler, count myself truly blessed!

June 1987

THE BRITISH CHARACTER
IMPORTANCE OF BEING ATHLETIC

KIND HEARTS AND CORONETS

'You will meet a tall dark stranger . . . then a short dark stranger . . . then a medium fair stranger . . . then a big fair stranger. . . then a small mousey stranger . . . then a small dark stranger . . .'

'I thought she usually sent a telegram.'

'It's an automatic factory-opener.'

Auberon Waugh

REGAL IMMIGRANTS

'Men will never be free until the last king is strangled with the entrails of the last priest,' wote Diderot, in his *Dithyrambe sur la fête de Roi*. Since then, men have had the opportunity to try out the new version of freedom which requires such grisly preparation. The general impression, one must admit, has not been too encouraging so far, and if the avoidance of such freedom requires us to keep the royal House of Schleswig-Holstein-Sonderburg-Glucksburg (alias Mountbatten alias Mountbatten-Windsor) in the style to which it is accustomed, then it seems a small price to pay.

On the face of it, a lively lad like Charles Schleswig-Holstein-Sonderburg-Glucksburg (alias Mountbatten-Windsor), our popular Prince of Wales, should not find it too difficult to avoid priestly entrails. It is not the sort of risk that many of us worry about. We may fall down an open manhole cover and be processed into de-activated sludge; we may be carried off by a golden eagle and fed to its ravenous young. But the chance of being strangled by a priest's entrails seems agreeably remote.

On the other hand, I can remember an occasion when I was given charge of four armoured cars on Salisbury Plain. You would have thought that with 120 square miles of Salisbury Plain lying empty before them, they could have avoided a collision. In the course of three hours, we had five collisions; two of the armoured cars were taken away for repairs and one was written off. I know perfectly well that if I were King

of England and there was only one priest left in the Kingdom, I would somehow get myself tangled up in his entrails.

But we all expect a higher standard of agility from the Royal House of Schleswig. Just as one goes to Italy for ice-creams, to Switzerland for cuckoo-clocks, so one goes to Germany for Kings and Queens. No English Royal House would have lasted half so long. Most of its members would have emigrated by now, in search of higher wages, less taxation and better opportunities abroad. Those left would be on strike half the time, or have relapsed into the sort of peculiarly English inertia which can only be distinguished from death by highly paid laboratory assistants on the National Health Service.

There is only one danger facing the British monarchy that I can see, and this is that it should become Anglicised and succumb to the English disease. When King George VI as Duke of York married the Lady Elizabeth Bowes-Lyon nobody may have noticed it at the time, as he was not heir to the throne, but he was introducing the first drop of English blood into the Royal Family for over three hundred years. The Queen Mother's immediate family, of course, is Scottish, but one has only to look at her father's pedigree and that of her mother to find a swarm of unmistakeably English names: Webb, Browne, Burnaby, Roland, Tucker, Hodgson, Smith, Walsh, Grimstead, Carpenter – all (or nearly all) English and all commoners.

Now the English are good at many things – they make the best shotguns in the world – but they are perfectly rotten at being Kings or Queens. It is for this reason that since King Harold we have always gone to France or Wales, or Scotland, or Holland or (when we could finally afford it) to Germany for our reigning monarchs. This unprecedented injection of English blood could only weaken the monarchy, and it was with enormous relief that one learned of the present Queen's engagement to Prince Philip (alias Mountbatten) allegedly from Greece, formerly of Denmark, but actually from Schleswig and Holstein and Sonderburg and Glucksburg and Beck. His other ancestors come from Schlieben, from the house of Hesse-Cassel, from Nassau-Usingen, from Mecklenburg-Schwerin, from Wurtemberg, from Prussia, from Mecklenburg-Strelitz, from Saxe-Altenburg, from Nassau-Weilburg, Battenberg, Baden, Saxe-Coburg-Gotha and a thousand other fairy-tale castles dotted around northern Europe, but whatever may be said against him he hasn't the tiniest trace of English blood.

Nor, of course, did his father-in-law, King George VI (of Saxe-Coburg-Gotha, alias Windsor), and a better king never drew breath. The present Queen has managed to keep all the Webbs, Brownes and Burnabys in her blood under strict control. But what about her son?

From his earlier years, when Cherry Brandy Charlie first hit the headlines at Gordonstoun, I have had the gravest misgivings about this young man. No doubt he would make the best possible companion on a desert island. I would buy a second-hand car from him without hesitation. But has he got the concentrated humourlessness, the severity, the ability to suffer fools endlessly and snub any hint of impertinence or forwardness which are essential to a thorough-going British monarch?

It is not that Germans have no sense of humour. They have a terrific sense of fun in many respects, and laugh as much as we do. It is just that their sense of humour is different. In an encouraging article which appeared in last November's *Books and Bookmen*, Prince Charles argued that his great-great-great-grandmother Queen Victoria was really a very humorous lady because she laughed whenever a man's trousers fell down while he was standing to attention. So far, so good. Prince Albert might

have laughed in these circumstances, even Dr George Steiner. But a true Englishman finds the sight of a man standing to attention irresistibly comical even if his trousers don't fall down. And it is this fatal flaw which has always disqualified the English from their own top job.

If ever a reigning monarch were to perceive the excellent practical joke which is being played on him night and day by the entire English nation, then it goes without saying that the joke would turn sour and the monarchy would collapse. I *think* the secret is safe from Prince Charles. We know he sees *Punch*, which is surely a good sign. We know he thinks his great-great-great-grandmother (a Hanoverian lady whose mother, bless her, came from Saxe-Coburg Saalfeld) had a terrific sense of humour, which is even better. We see him from time to time wearing a lavatory seat around his head, which could scarcely bode fairer. But what about his children?

In twenty-five years' time the Queen will be 76 and I think it fair to assume that she will have retired from the throne, in one way or another. Queen Victoria would never have dreamed of retiring, of course, but we must remember that Queen Elizabeth II is nearly a quarter English, having a grandmother who was born Miss Smith and a great-grandmother born Miss Hodgson. Prince Charles will be a mature 54 years old, and almost certainly thinking hard about his own retirement. And his children? I hope I am giving away no secrets if I hazard the guess that his eldest child will already be over 21.

If he persists in his determination to marry an Englishwoman, I can see no future for the British monarchy. Time and again he has refused my advice to go to the Royal House of Saudi Arabia for his bride. Why doesn't he even go to Germany like everyone else? Perhaps he thinks we can no longer afford a German girl, but I'm sure Mr Healey could raise another loan.

On 18 November 1760 King George III inaugurated this great English joke when he declared from the steps of the throne in his heavy German accent, 'Born and educated in zis country, I glory in ze name of Briton.' Prince Charles threatens to bring it to an end by marrying the first Englishwoman to sit on the British throne since Catharine Parr. It goes without saying that nobody who was half English could possibly read the Royal Speech opening any Parliament with a straight face. Make no mistake about it, such a hybrid would be sure to tangle in the first priest's entrails it met. If the monarchy goes, we will have no defence left against the mean, bossy, incompetent proletarian future which threatens us even now. I beg him to think again.

January 1977

Hugh Chesterman
THE FALLIBLES

'CANUTE,' his flattering courtiers cried,
'Can do what he likes with the rising tide;'
But he only wetted his feet when he tried.

ALFRED THE GREAT was most discerning;
He kindled and trimmed the Lamp of
    Learning;
But he couldn't prevent a cake from burning.

WILLIAM THE RED was no cock-sparrow
But a fighting man to his Norman marrow;
Yet he hadn't the wit to dodge an arrow.

JOHN, an experienced evil liver,
Knew how to make his subjects shiver;
But he lost his handbag crossing a river.

PREHISTORIC PEEPS
'NO BATHING TO-DAY!'

RICHARD THE THIRD was crowned, and he
Swore that a careful King he'd be;
Yet he lost his crown on a hawthorn-tree.

HENRY THE EIGHTH was a real tip-topper,
Slick with his tongue and quick with the
    chopper;
Yet he came (too oft) a connubial cropper.

CHARLES was a ruler born and bred,
Cool and collected; yet I've read
That once he completely lost his head.
So it's nice to know that even kings
Can make a mess of the simplest things.

July 1929

W. C. Sellar and R. J. Yeatman

1066 AND ALL THAT

*[Being extracts from a forthcoming
History of England (Absit Oman)]*

CÆSAR INVADES BRITAIN

The first date in English History is 55 B.C.,
in which year JULIUS CÆSAR (the memorable
Roman Emperor) landed, like all other successful invaders of these islands, at Thanet.
This was in the olden days when the Romans
were top nation on account of their classical
education, etc.

JULIUS CÆSAR advanced very energetically, throwing his cavalry several thousands
of paces over the River Flumen; but the
Ancient Britons, though all well over military age, painted themselves true blue, or
woad, and fought as heroically under their
dashing queen, BOADICEA, as they did later

in thin red lines under their good queen,
VICTORIA.

JULIUS CÆSAR was therefore compelled to
invade Britain again the following year
(54 B.C., not 56, owing to the peculiar Roman
method of counting), and having defeated
the Ancient Britons by unfair means, such
as battering-rams, tortoises, hippocausts,
centipedes, axes and bundles, set the memorable Latin sentence, '*Veni, Vidi, Vici,*'
which the Romans, who were all very well
educated, construed correctly.

The Britons, however, who of course still
used the old pronunciation, understanding
him to have called them 'Weeny, Weedy and
Weaky,' lost heart and gave up the struggle,
thinking that he had already divided them
all into three parts and had thus won the war.

The Roman Conquest was, however, a
Good Thing, since the Britons were only
natives at that time.

THE ROMAN OCCUPATION

For some reason the Romans neglected to
overrun the country with fire and the sword,
though they had both of these; in fact after
the Conquest they did not mingle with the
Britons at all, but lived a semi-detached life
in villas. They occupied their time for two
or three hundred years in building Roman
roads and having Roman baths. The Roman
roads ran absolutely straight in all directions
and all led to Rome.

The Romans also built a wall between
England and Scotland to keep out the savage
Picts and Scots. This wall was the work of
the memorable Roman Emperor BALBUS and
was thus called HADRIAN'S Wall. The Picts,
or painted men,* were so called to dis-
tinguish them from the Britons. (*Vide supra,
Woad.*)

---

* *E.g.* The Black Watch, the Red Comyn and Doug-
lases of all colours.

'Are you going down to tell them, or shall I?'

BRITAIN CONQUERED AGAIN

The withdrawal of the Roman legions to take part in GIBBONS' *Decline and Fall of the Roman Empire* left Britain defenceless and subjected to that long succession of Waves of which history is chiefly composed. While the Roman Empire was overrun by Waves not only of Ostrogoths, Visigoths and even Goths but also of Vandals (who destroyed works of art) and Huns (who destroyed everything), Britain was attacked by Waves of Picts (and, of course, Scots), who had recently learnt how to climb the wall, and of Angles Saxons and Jutes, who, landing at Thanet, soon overran the country with fire (and, of course, the sword).

IMPORTANT NOTE

The Scots (originally Irish, but by now Scotch) were at this time inhabiting Ireland, having driven the Irish (Picts) out of Scotland; while the Picts (originally Scots) were now Irish (living in brackets) and *vice versa*. It is essential to keep these distinctions clearly in mind.

HUMILIATION OF THE BRITONS

The brutal Saxon invaders drove the Britons westward into Wales and compelled them to become Welsh; it is now considered doubtful whether this was a *Good Thing*. The country became almost entirely inhabited by Saxons and was therefore renamed England and thus (naturally) soon became C. of E. This was a *Good Thing*, because previously the Saxons had worshipped some dreadful gods of their own called Monday, Tuesday, Wednesday, Thursday, Friday and Saturday.

ETHELRED THE UNREADY. A WEAK KING

ETHELRED THE UNREADY was the first Weak King of England. He was called the Unready because he was never ready when the Danes were. Rather than wait for him the Danes used to fine him large sums called Danegeld for not being ready. But though they were always ready the Danes had very bad memories and often used to forget that they had been paid the Danegeld and come back for it almost before they had sailed away. By that time ETHELRED was always unready again.

Finally, ETHELRED was taken completely unawares by his own death and was succeeded by CANUTE.

CANUTE, AN EXPERIMENTAL KING

This memorable monarch, having set out from Norway to collect some Danegeld, landed by mistake at Thanet and thus became King. He began by being a Bad King on the advice of his courtiers, who informed him (owing to a misunderstanding of the Rule Britannia) that the King of England was entitled to sit in the sea without getting wet. But having proved that they were wrong he decided to take his own advice in future and became a Good King and C. of E., and ceased to be memorable.

After CANUTE there were no more aquatic kings till WILLIAM IV.

CANUTE had two sons, Halfacanute and Partacanute, and two other offspring, Rathacanute and Hardlicanute, whom however he would never acknowledge, denying to the last that he was their Fathacanute.

TEST PAPER
Up to 1066

1. Discuss, in Latin or Gothic (*but not both*), whether the Northumbrian Bishops were more schismatical than the Cumbrian Abbots. (Be bright.)

2. Which came first, A.D. or B.C.? (Be careful.)

3. Has it never occurred to you that the Romans *counted backwards*? (Be honest.)

4. How angry would you be if it was suggested –
   (*a*) That the XIth Chap. of the *Consolations of Boethius* was an interpolated palimpsest?
   (*b*) That an Eisteddfod was an agricultural implement?

5. Have you the faintest recollection of –
   (*a*) Ethelbreth?
   (*b*) Athelthral?
   (*c*) Thruthelthrolth?

6. What *have* you the faintest recollection of?

7. Estimate the average age of
   (*a*) The Ancient Britons.
   (*b*) Ealdormen.
   (*c*) Old King Cole.

8. Why do you know nothing at all about
   (*a*) The Laws of Infangthief and Eggseisin?
   (*b*) Saint Pancras?

N.B. – Do not attempt to answer more than one question at a time.

WILLIAM I: A CONQUERING KING

In the year 1066 occurred the other memorable date in English History, viz., *William the Conqueror, Ten sixty-six*. This is also called *The Battle of Hastings*, and was when WILLIAM I (1066) conquered England at the Battle of Senlac (*Ten sixty-six*).

The Norman Conquest was a *Good Thing*, as from this time onwards England stopped being conquered and thus was able to become top nation.

DOOMSDAY BOOK

WILLIAM invented a system according to which everybody had to belong to somebody else, and everybody else to the King. This was called the Feutile System, and in order to prove that it was true he wrote a book called the *Doomsday Book*, which contained an inventory of all the Possessions of all his subjects. After reading the book through carefully WILLIAM agreed with it and signed it, indicating to everybody that the Possessions mentioned in it were now his.

Although WILLIAM THE CONQUEROR (1066) was a very strong King he was eventually stumbled to death by a horse and was succeeded by his son RUFUS.

HENRY I: A Tragic King

HENRY I was famous for his handwriting and was therefore generally called Henry Beau-geste. He was extremely fond of his son WILLIAM, who was, however, drowned. HENRY tried to console himself for his loss by eating a surfeit of palfreys. This was a *Bad Thing* since he died of it and, in fact, *never smiled again*.

HENRY II: A JUST KING

HENRY II was a great lawgiver, and it was he who laid down the great Legal Principle that

'Even if it's only a short crusade, don't forget –
Clunk, Click!'

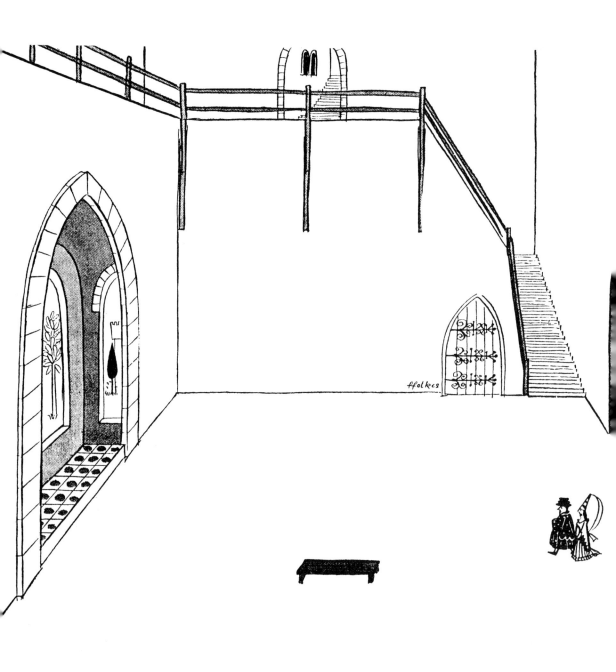

'I'm afraid we rather counted too much on our wedding presents to furnish the place.'

everything is either legal or (preferably) illegal. He also made another very just arrangement about trials.

Before HENRY II's time there were two kinds of legal trial: (*a*) the Ideal and (*b*) the Combat. The Ideal form of trial consisted in making a man plunge his head in boiling ploughshares in order to see whether he had committed a crime or not. According to HENRY's reformed system a man was tried first by a jury of his equals and only had to plunge his head into the ploughshares afterwards (in order to confirm the jury's opinion that he was either innocent or had committed the crime).

This was obviously a much *Better Thing*.

The Combat was a system by which in civil cases the litigants decided their dispute by mortal combat, after which the defeated party was allowed to fly the country. But HENRY altered all this and declared that a Grand Jury must decide first what the parties were fighting about – a reform which naturally gave rise to grave discontent among the Barons, who believed in the Combat, the whole Combat and nothing but the Combat.

September 1930

Miles Kington

THE QUEEN'S PACIFIC DIARY

Feb 11

Arrived in Western Samoa. The landscape is very like, well, like Eastern Samoa. Palm trees, blue skies and lots of sunshine. I took care to rub in my Jubilee sun tan lotion and put on my Jubilee sun glasses, as worn by myself, before venturing out in to the morning glare. My timetable on the first day of my grand tour of the Pacific was very exacting. Just to give you an example, here is the schedule for my first hour.

9.00 am Arrive and avoid customs but fail to avoid Samoan dignitaries and handshakes.

9.03 Visit local school and am presented with Jubilee gift made of palm leaves.

9.06 Tour of capital. Meet mayor and am presented with Jubilee gift made of coconut shells. Shake hands with 400 Samoan officials, many of them much stronger than I am.

9.11 Meet harbourmaster and his entire staff, who present me with Jubilee trophy made of sea shells. Absent-mindedly present him with palm and coconut gifts just received.

9.13 Declare new Jubilee bus shelter open.

9.15 Declare another two Jubilee bus shelters open. Remark jokingly to official that bus shelters always seem to come along in groups of three or four. He shakes hand and says nothing. Usual firm, direct grip; I must be the only person who looks forward to people with limp, pallid handshakes.

9.21 Am shown round main factory in Samoa, which seems to make nothing but Jubilee handicraft. I shake hands with factory manager, forty workers and a coat-stand. Am presented with Jubilee gift made from sharks' teeth. I think it is either a back-scratcher or, on the other hand, not a back-scratcher. Philip says it would make a lovely stock if boiled up.

9.27 Caught in the island's only traffic jam. Stand and wave radiantly to Samoan crowds.

9.33 Still caught in traffic jam.

9.37 I declare the traffic jam officially open and make a short speech urging brotherhood among those caught in traffic jams. Shake hands with many passers-by and am presented with Jubilee programmes to sign. Refuse offer gracefully.

9.42 Meet harbourmaster and his entire staff again. Apparent mix-up in arrangements. I greet him regally and ask him how he has been since I last saw him. Much embarrassed, he casts around for another gift and presents me with his chart of the harbour. Cannot help feeling the harbour will be full of wrecked ships before long. I present him with a stand-by rolled up document.

9.54 Arrive at college to give speech to massed students. Find I have given speech to harbourmaster. I give Christmas broadcast 1971 version, remembering just in time to omit reference to coming Olympic Games, but unfortunately failing to omit references to Northern Ireland.

9.59 I present diplomas to graduating students, not daring to look and see if I am giving away more speeches. One hefty student gives me unusually strong handshake. I forget myself and instinctively crush his hand. When you shake hands as often as I do, you could wrist wrestle anyone to the ground.

Feb 12

Am giving up vain attempt to log my life day by day, as it would take two hours or 600 handshakes, or half a Samoan banquet as given on the beach last night. (See menu attached: Jubilee soup very good, roast Jubilee sucking pig very good, Jubilee pudding terrible. Heaven knows what they put in the Jubilee coffee but had awful headache this morning.) But at least it shows that I am working like a beaver, as Mr Jack Jones has urged us all to do. Poor Mr Jones was embarrassed by poll which showed that 54% of the British think he has more power than the Premier. He is in a kind of constitutional position not unlike our own. I would not call him radiant, but feel he has great dignity.

Philip says, what would Oliver Twist say if he was King of England.

'I do not know,' I say, as I always do to get it over with. 'What would he say?'

'Please, sir, I want Samoa.'

Feb 13

Shook hands, smiled, gave speech, was sorry about earthquake. I now have fifty-eight gifts made of palm leaves. Surprised to see so many trees left standing on island.

Spotted a Jubilee tee-shirt for the first time. The portrait of me is insufferable. It is bad enough not being able to recognise myself on stamps and pennies; when I cannot recognise myself on men's chests, I give up. The trouble is with this Jubilee that it is all out of my control. All other great marketing operations, like Snoopy objects or Beatles trivia, can be controlled by Mr Schulz or Apple; I have to sit by and watch my face being put on drinking vessels and like it. What Philip calls, one silly mug put on another.

Oh for the Queen Trading and Marketing Corporation!

Bad news from home. Lots of rain and snow, and Our Park Rangers have lost away again.

Feb 14

St Valentine's Day. An anonymous Jubilee mug through the post. I thanked Philip for it. I do not know what I would do without his unfailing good humour.

Feb 15

It strikes me that the people of these islands are much more monarchist than the British. I do not blame the Scots and Welsh for being anti-monarchist; being of predominantly German and Scottish blood myself, I too despair of the way the English handle things. But you would think the English might be a bit more pro-monarchy; if it were not for Mr

Willie Hamilton stirring up feeling in my favour, there might be no reaction at all.

On the other hand, the Tongans have a monarch already.

I looked up beaver in the encyclopaedia today. I am not sure I ought to be working like one. Apparently it merely despoils the landscape till it has made a home and then sits back and rests.

Feb 16

Apparently we are now in Fiji. I do not remember arriving. But we were given a marvellous reception. I opened two schools and a hospital and a banquet. I often wonder if they keep schools and hospitals closed on purpose until I arrive. Is there also, I wonder, an upsurge in the standard of education and health when I have visited a place? 'Jubilee O Levels at record height this year.' 'Queen rids isles of croup and measles.'

I wish I knew who had leaked that story about making Philip the Prince Consort to Nigel Dempster. Awful to think that one's relations need money from the *Daily Mail*. Perhaps I should always offer to up his bid by £10.

Philip says, why don't I spike Dempster's guns by giving *him* an official title. He suggests the Raconteur Royal. I would give him open access to my files in return for an undertaking not to print certain stories. I am not sure about this.

Fijians amazingly loyal. It would be so nice to flee to Fiji like Mr Gauguin to Tahiti. Raising corgis on a romantic South Seas dog ranch ... but I must not have dreams like this.

Mar 1

I have been in New Zealand for ten days now and have never seen so many sheep in my life.

I must admit that I fell briefly asleep during a ceremony yesterday morning, which Philip puts down to my counting sheep morning, noon and night.

Today is St David's Day, which made me think of the Prince of Wales. I really think it is about time he settled down to a career. Always in and out of some armed force or other. Or attending a Goon Show revival. Or keeping one girl-friend ahead of the *Daily Mail*.

'Why can't he take up something professionally like you?' I asked Philip.

'You mean, being Prince Consort?' he inquired.

'No – writing introductions for books,' I quipped.

'I make the jokes round here,' he said darkly.

Mar 8

Our second day in Australia. The Australians are very like the New Zealanders, except that there are many more of them, which explains why they fight more in queues and are more pushy. It is the only country I know where I find myself shaking hands with *three* people simultaneously.

Our meeting with Sir John Kerr was not a pleasant one. I knew he was unpopular in Australia but had not expected to see so many eggs thrown, especially as several of them came from Philip – still, he always enters the spirit of any occasion. But I felt constrained to leave when the lager tins started flying, and was only partly mollified by the fact that they contained Jubilee lager.

One heckler shouted with typical Aussie crudeness: 'Go home, Lizzie!'

'OK' Philip shouted back, 'if you'll take Rolf Harris in exchange!'

Enormous popularity has ensued.

Mar 9

Huge crowds now turn up to hear Philip's

repartee to heckling. This afternoon we were opening a new lager factory next door to a cricket stadium somewhere in Queensland, or Ourland as I like to think of it, and someone yelled, 'Why's the Queen come here to Australia, eh?' and Philip shouted back, 'To save you from Edna Everage!'

Afterwards, he explained to me who Edna Everage was. From the sound of her, anything she can do, I can do better.

'Listen, darling – our tune.'

We have been offered our own show on Australian TV.

Mar 15

New poll in Britain shows that 64 per cent of population are now apathetic about monarchy, and God knows I can't help agreeing with them. It coincides with secret offer to move permanently to Australia, New Zealand etc, as Queen of the South Seas. This is a pleasant thought, but I have to tell secret emissary that it is quite out of the question.

'Plus,' he says, 'we will give you full control over all Jubilee merchandise, plus chance to answer back all critics on TV, plus full immigration ban on Nigel Dempster.'

This changes matter completely. I will think about it and give the answer in tomorrow's diary entry.

January 1977

'I'm not disappointed exactly – it's just that from your portrait in fireworks I'd expected somebody taller.'

Basil Boothroyd

BY APPOINTMENT

In 1969 Basil Boothroyd was commissioned to write the biography of the Duke of Edinburgh.

'Well, Hello,' said Lt-Commander Slater, RN, greeting me cheerfully on the squelching lawn. 'Come inside and meet the Queen.' It was one of Norfolk's wetter mornings.

Coming inside didn't mean Sandringham House, where the royal car from King's Lynn station had sped on after dropping me, but Wood Farm, a cottagey outpost on the estate. Sizeable as cottages go, but in a state of comfortable disorder: convenient that day as a base for the shooting; at other times when Prince Philip or members of his family fancied a short escape on their own without the fuss and expense of opening up the house.

In fact I met the Queen Mother first, not at once identifiable, perched on the arm of a chair in a bundled-up looking macintosh of some iridescent fabric and a hat in poor shape. She was welcoming and apologetic. 'How awful to drag you up here in this weather!' It was no worse, I said, on an ungraceful impulse, than being landed in the lap of the Royal Family. She laughed. 'I shouldn't worry about that. Jock, why hasn't he got a drink?'

The Lt-Commander was Jock. To all, including me within a few hours. The Queen's equerry, but at everyone's bidding.

'Jock,' Princess Anne was later to call across the tea table, 'why no kipper pâté?'

He nodded gravely, and ostentatiously tied a knot in his handkerchief.

I leaned on him heavily that weekend. He answered all my nervous questions. Mealtimes, tipping, who was who in the rest of the party, right up to my closing doubts about the thank-you letter. Prince Philip had invited me. The Queen was my hostess. 'Oh, do write to her,' said Jock. 'She loves getting them.' I worried about addressing the envelope. 'Just put "The Queen" and send it to me. I'll see she gets it.' It all seemed agreeably casual.

But even he could hardly help with the writing. I scrapped several drafts, including one with something about having been entertained royally.

One of the things I asked him was whether someone could be found to drive me round the estate on the Sunday afternoon. He tied a mental knot in his handkerchief, and presently came to my room to say the Land-Rover was at the door, which it was, Prince Philip waiting at the wheel without noticeable impatience. Jock had found someone.

Inside the crowded sitting-room at Wood Farm my hostess soon approached, in jeans and an orange jumper and stepping over retrievers. 'I'm afraid,' were her first words, 'we seem to have an enormous lot of dogs in here.' What did I say? That that was perfectly all right?

Somehow and suddenly we were then discussing aircraft noises over Windsor, and I am sure I sympathised. Residents in the Castle apparently suffer not a little from the sitings of Heathrow runways.

Prince Charles struggled from behind a sofa. 'I knew I was right. I thought it was you.' This, I felt, was something he had been looking forward to.

We moved into lunch. More properly lunches, since the party was divided in two. Prince Charles and Princess Anne (headscarf, weathered jeans) took their party into some room beyond. The Queen and Prince Philip stayed with mine. He had first drawn my attention to photographs on the walls from his book *Birds from Britannia*, ending with one on the inside of the loo door. 'My favourite.' It was of some bird squatting low on its nest in an attitude of strain.

I forget what we ate. Something unremarkable. 'I think,' said Prince Philip, after helping me to decide about vegetables, 'you might try to get something into the book about my family. Not much is known about them. They were quite interesting people.' A remark later to lead me into the tangled branches of royal trees. Monkey-puzzles. I could already see, even starting from the graspable fact that George V, Kaiser Wilhelm II, Tsar Nicholas II and Prince Andrew of Greece (Prince Philip's father), were all

'Well, we ought to take them something.'

first cousins, and Grand Duchess Olga of Russia was his maternal grandmother, that this was going to be something more challenging than articles about Celia and the Washing-up.

He thought I might usefully talk to his sisters, Princess Sophie of Hanover and Princess Margarita of Greece. 'Usefully' was one of his words. He was always thinking of useful approaches. No insistence. Possibilities opened. The sisters lived in Bavaria.

'Would they talk to me?'

'Of course.'

Just a matter of fixing up to meet them somewhere. Munich, say.

I could get lost in Munich. To some degree I was lost already. February was imminent. The book was to be out before June 10 next year. I am a slow writer. I go to wrong airports. I hate research.

And as yet not a word on paper.

The invitation had come informally enough, by telephone from the palace. 'The boss thinks you might find a weekend at Sandringham useful. How about the one after next?'

I think the speaker was Bill Heseltine, then the Queen's press officer, now Sir William and her Private Secretary. A man of endearing openness and daunting intelligence, he was to be the smoother of all my paths. But it may have been Major Randle Cooke, the Duke's equerry at the time, and another rock of support. Whoever it was, I was given a selection of trains to King's Lynn: and asked my size in wellingtons, which of course would be supplied. Details are looked after in those circles.

My first thought on receiving an invitation of any kind is how to get out of it. I would have paid money to get out of this one. There was no way. When I came back from the telephone and told my wife we rivalled each other for pallor.

I dwelt gratefully on the wellingtons during the lunch at Wood Farm. The rain still fell, and was to continue during the next three hours of bogged-down walking under slaty skies. It was my first and last shoot. At least I was not to participate actively. It had not been suggested that I should bring a gun, though for all anyone present knew I could have been a lifelong, twelve-bore man and the terror of every fowl that flew. While various of the royalty and nobility banged away, I mostly trudged beside Lady Rose Baring, lady-in-waiting and companionable soul. I confided my haziness about Sandringham, how it was run, staffed, paid for.

'You must talk to Charlie,' she said. 'He's coming to tea.'

'Charlie?' I said. 'It's all very well for you lot, loosing off these first names. But for a visitor from outer space ...'

She was laughingly abject. 'It isn't fair to do that, I do see.' Charlie was Lord Tryon, holder of the Privy Purse-strings.

An area having been shot over, there were intermittent rushes for the convoy of cars, jeeps, pick-ups, beaters' vans, suddenly moving on, as if at a secret signal, to the next scene of uneven contest. I sometimes had to board briskly or get left behind, and once scrambled into the back of something already moving to share it with the Queen and a muddy dog, both invincibly cheerful.

No conversation sprang readily to mind. The weather, perhaps? Or I could have asked what entertainment was derived from these exercises by a fellow non-participant.

It was the one-on-one dialogue that always gave me most pause. Walking down the long corridor to my room on one occasion I saw that I should have to pass my hostess, cutting up dog-food at some sideboardly piece of furniture. I could have said, 'Hello,' which would be familiar. Bowed, which would have gone unseen. Pretended not to notice. Disrespectful. But I plumped for that in the end.

Things were easier at mealtimes, even at

tea, without benefit of alcohol. More people, more talk.

Tea would be 'immediate', said Jock, as the party finally queued up at the House for a hand-wind bootscraper (said to have been an invention of Prince Philip's, but I never pinned him down on that).

'Come and sit by me,' said the Queen, patting a chair and pouring tea from something almost urnlike, in silver and on spindles. I understood the size of the teapot as the company drifted in. We ended up with a dozen or so, Prince Philip last and opposite, Princess Anne on my other side, Lord Tryon, the Keeper of the Privy Purse, also at our end. The rest, so to speak, nowhere.

This was a family tea, a spread of scones, toast, jam, cucumber sandwiches, chocolate biscuits wrapped or unwrapped, fruit-cake, sponge layer cake, several assorted pâtés – though no kipper. Princess Anne went on at Slater somewhat, in mock-complaint, even

after his handkerchief knot. 'I mean, why not?' 'I don't see. We did have kippers for breakfast.' They exchanged grimaces.

When the first cup left base I passed it on to her. She passed it back. 'The big ones are for the men. There's no women's lib in this place.' I suppose I looked questioning. 'Actually, the real reason is just that we haven't enough of this service to go round.'

On my left, my offer of cake was graciously declined. The Queen thought that would not be 'at all wise', and didn't eat much of anything, was partly preoccupied with a couple of hungry Corgis and a threat to stockings (having changed into short yellow dress), partly with some argument opposite, where her husband was pressing Tryon to release funds for the refurbishing of houses on the estate. Tryon resisting. The Queen supporting him. 'Don't you rise to it.'

Tomorrow was Sunday. The talk moved on to ecclesiastical undermanning. Five local

'I don't know quite how to tell you this, dearest Albert, but it seems you're not going to make the Jubilee.'

livings, three of them in the Queen's gift, two in other people's. How could they get together and work out something? At present, only two priests for five churches.

'So you see,' said Prince Philip, drawing me in, 'there are some Sundays when some of them don't have services.'

'Yes, they do, darling.'

'No, they don't.'

'Yes, they do. It only means that if Flitcham has matins, then Sandringham can only have Communion – Oh, Jock, you will go along tomorrow to see the church is warm? Last week in the hymns our breath was going out like trumpets.' Tea over, the Queen and the Earl of Westmorland departed together, in an atmosphere faintly conspiratorial, disappearing into some kind of antechamber. Prince Charles wanted to show some old silent film comedies. 'I don't know,' said his father, rising on a sigh. 'Your films. And my in-tray's overflowing.'

We all saw them eventually, Prince Philip with enthusiasm, putting words into the wordless lips and chiding those dead comics for standing in the line of hosepipes and custard-pies which they could easily have evaded.

Prince Charles had taken station at the door of the ballroom, and ushered us in. I said, 'I thought you were taking the money.' Was this a thing to say? Too late now.

'Forty-seven! Did you hear that, Your Majesty? Sir Francis has beaten the old record by a clear ten ferrets!'

'All contributions gratefully received,' said the usher. As the rest of us broke up from the tea table, Jock had felt it among his duties to explain about the vanished Queen and Earl. 'It's all a bit comical.' Westmorland, it seemed, long a Lord in Waiting, was to become a KCVO. This, even for an earl, involved knighting.

'If we'd been at the palace, there would have been a great ceremonial to-do. Lord Chamberlain, all the Household, me in my uniform with aiguillettes and all. But as he's been asked down here to get it, and to shoot into the bargain, she just takes him next door and does it.'

The couple presently reappeared, the new knight a little pink. There were handshakes. 'What's happening?' someone asked. 'David's just been knighted,' said somebody else. 'Yes,' said the Queen. 'I've dubbed him.' A mischievous inflexion on the 'dubbed', and her transforming laugh.

Monday's *Times* carried the formal announcement.

June 1987

Lord Mancroft

MY TRIBE, RIGHT OR WRONG

Down in the other place (which is the delicate way in which the Lords refer to the Commons) they had a debate recently on standards of behaviour in the City of London. It was rather a pointed little debate, with some quite sharp comments on the tribal customs of Threadneedle Street. 'Cor,' I thought to myself, 'look who's talking!' If ever there was a place that's larynx deep in tribal customs it's the Commons House of Parliament. Where else in the world would you find a Chief Whip raising a point of order during the course of a debate by crawling across the floor of the House wearing a battered, moth-eaten opera-hat? And in what other legislative chamber, if you wanted the debate to continue in secret, would you get up and declare that you spied strangers?

There's tribal customs for you with a vengeance! But I must be careful what I say because up our end of the corridor, in the Lords, we also have our tribal customs and one of the most serious is the custom that discourages us from putting out our tongue at the Commons. It doesn't always operate vice quite so versa and you've no idea how bluff the Commons can be to the Lords when they're in a reforming frame of mind.

I'm a keen man for tribal customs myself; indeed, I'm a whole-hearted tribalist. Some people are great joiners – I believe that the late Sir Harry Britain joined over 200 clubs in his time, a large number of which he invented himself and many of which will not survive him for long. Well, I can't really say that I actually joined the House of Lords. I just edged my way in when my father died 35 years ago and I was able to produce the requisite piece of vellum arguing in some pretty ripe language that I was his heir male lawfully begotten. My mother said why didn't somebody talk it over with her instead of wasting the time of the Clerk of the Parliaments but I explained to her that tribal customs, rather than sweet reasonableness, had to be observed and I was now a member of one of the world's most exclusive tribes.

I was made aware of this exclusivity at an early stage of my membership. You're not supposed to cross the floor of the House between the Woolsack and the Table when the Mace is in position. This, one day, I forgot. I crossed. Woe was me! The Lord Chancellor sent for me at once. 'I beg of you never to do that again,' he said sternly. 'I myself don't mind at all, but the Mace simply hates it.'

Mark you, tribal customs can change. When I first joined the House, there wasn't often a very cluttered attendance and the prearranged list of speakers was sparse. Any noble lord venturing to address the House after tea invariably began with the apologetic words, 'My Lords, at this late hour . . .' Nowadays, what with a couple of hundred new life peers and an attendance allowance of £13.50 *per diem*, you'll get a Speaker's list of about 25 even on such a measure as the Aberdeen Harbour (Sludge Removal) Confirmation Order Bill. And some very poignant oratory that might produce too. The Scottish Peers can be particularly tribal when they feel in the mood.

To Students of Tribal Infallibility, the House of Lords offers a fascinating case study. To begin with, the rights of several different tribes are intertwined within our ritual. I myself am an entrenched member of many tribes, not least the Law and the Army, whose tribal customs frequently mingle with those of the Lords. When, for instance, FM the Earl Montgomery of Alamein addressed their lordships (more regularly, alas, then he does now) he was pained to find that the Crossbenchers and the maturer Liberal Peers did not react quite so sharply to his oratory as the recruit squads of the Royal Warwickshire Regiment had reacted to Colonel Montgomery's exhortations in days gone by. Nor did he relish the observation of a Durham Coalmining Peer that, unlike the Bourbons, Monty had learned nothing and forgotten everything.

Durham Coalmining Peers bring up their own tribal customs when they are ennobled, but the speed with which they change their former revolutionary tendencies for the generally milder outlook of the House of Lords is touching. The lawyers re-adjust their tribalities more reluctantly and I say this myself as an erstwhile member of the legal tribe. The House of Lords is, of course, in itself two separate tribes, an upper Legislative Chamber and a Supreme Court. The Lords of Appeal in ordinary are members of both tribes and some of them re-adjust to the dual role more easily than others. Even Lord Goddard, when Lord Chief Justice, occasionally overlooked this point and tended to address the House in its Parliamentary Capacity as if their lordships were a jury of Gloucestershire pig-farmers. 'Come off it, Rayner,' exclaimed Lord Exeter, once, in his firmest Elizabethan tones, 'you're not in your damn police court now. You're addressing your Peers.' Even the formidable Rayner Goddard had to acknowledge a few tribal rules!

I myself have belonged to many other tribes besides those of the Lords, the law and the army. I suppose my first tribe, right or wrong, was the Nanny tribe, perambulating under the trees in Hyde Park, and although I was barely nine months old at the time, I remember the whole thing as if it were only yesterday. On this pram in which today two little Kuwaitis scream their heads off would have been blazoned a ducal coronet. On another, wherein now croons the heir to a High Street multiple store fortune, should have been displayed (all proper) the arms of a well-known earl and the legs of an even better known Gaiety Girl. The Tribal Chief (the Senior Nanny) sat knitting tricoteusely in our midst. She knew *Debrett* by heart and woe betide any junior nursemaid who put a foot out of line.

Thence, I progressed through the tribal rituals of prep school (hell), Winchester (literate sadism) and eventually up to Oxford (bliss).

Later came the Army, which, oddly

enough, I loved and whose tribalism, right or wrong, I will still defend to the death, though the army did put me on my guard, for all its tribalistic splendour, against the danger of taking all tribalism for granted. In my regiment, for instance, we drank the Loyal Toast with one foot on the table. Tradition has it that as we swung into the saddle for Quatre Bras, straight from our meal outside some rustic inn, our Colonel suddenly reminded us that we had not yet drunk the Loyal Toast. This we duly did – one foot still in the stirrup – and away we galloped; good Hollywood stuff.

It would have been tribally even more impressive, if I had not subsequently discovered that our Regiment was not raised until twenty years after Quatre Bras.

Nevertheless, my tribe; right or wrong.

Oh well! And the moral of this is, probably, let tribal rights lie. After all, even the House of Lords hasn't a completely clear conscience. When they first opened up the Woolsack at the turn of the century, in order to give it a good going-over, they discovered it was stuffed with cotton.

March 1976

'Heavens, no. I'm only the caretaker.'

THE BRITISH CHARACTER
PASSION FOR NOT FORGETTING THE MODERATELY GREAT

P. G. Wodehouse

PUT ME AMONG THE EARLS

A critic, with whose name I will not sully my typewriter, was giving me the sleeve across the windpipe the other day for including so many members of the Peerage in the casts of characters of my books. Specifically, he accused me of an undue fondness for Earls.

Well, of course, now that I come to tot up the score, I realise that in the course of my literary career I have featured quite a number of these fauna, but as I often say ... well, perhaps once a fortnight ... Why not? I see no objection to Earls. A most respectable class of men they seem to me. And one admires their spirit. I mean, while some, of course, have come up the easy way, many have had the dickens of a struggle, starting at the bottom of the ladder as mere Hons, having to go in to dinner after the Vice-Chancellor of the Duchy of Lancaster and all that sort of thing.

Show me the Hon who by pluck and determination has raised himself from the depths, step by step, till he becomes entitled to keep a coronet on the hat peg in the downstairs cupboard, and I will show you a man of whom any author might be proud to write.

Earls on the whole have made a very good showing in fiction. With Baronets setting them a bad example by being almost uniformly steeped in crime, they have preserved a gratifyingly high standard of behaviour. There is seldom anything wrong with the Earl in fiction, if you don't mind a touch of haughtiness and a tendency to have heavy eyebrows and draw them together in a formidable frown, like the one in Little Lord Fauntleroy. And in real life I can think of almost no Earls whose hearts were not as pure and fair as those of dwellers in the lowlier air of Seven Dials.

Oh yes. Earl Carroll. He caused a lot of talk in New York some years ago by giving a party at which a girl took a bath in champagne with, if I have the story rightly, not so much as a Bikini bathing-suit on. But he was not a member of the Peerage, he was a theatrical producer. (That is a thing you have to be careful of in America. Earl is a Christian name.)

Our literature, lacking Earls, would have been a great deal poorer. Shakespeare would have been lost without them. Everyone who has written for the theatre knows how difficult it is to get people off the stage unless you can think of a good exit speech. That is why, as you pass through Bloomsbury and other literary quarters, you see haggard men wandering about and sticking straws in their hair as they mutter:

'Life, dear lady ...'
'Life, dear lady, is like ...'

'Dear lady, I have but two objections to life. One is that it ...'

Than which nothing is sadder.

Shakespeare had no such problem. With more Earls than he knew what to do with, he was on velvet. One need only quote those well-known lines from his *Henry the Seventh,* Part One:

My lord of Sydenham, bear our royal word
To Brixton's Earl, the Earl of Wormwood
 Scrubs,
Our faithful liege, the Earl of Dulwich
 (East),
And those of Beckenham, Penge and
 Peckham Rye,
Together with the Earl of Hampton Wick:
Bid them to haste like cats when struck
 with brick,
For they are needed in our battle line,
And stitch in time doth ever save full nine.
 [*Exeunt Omnes. Trumpets and hautboys.*]

'Pie!' Shakespeare used to say to Burbage as he slapped the stuff down, and Burbage would agree that Shakespeare earned his money easily.

A thing about Earls I have never understood, and never liked to ask anyone for fear of betraying my ignorance, is why one Earl is the Earl of Whoosis and another Earl just Earl Smith. I always think Earl Smith sounds a bit abrupt, almost like a nickname. I have an idea – I may be wrong – that the 'of' boys have a slight social edge on the others, like the aristocrats in Germany who are able to call themselves 'Von.' One can picture the Earl of Brighton being introduced to Earl Hove at a cocktail party. The host says 'Oh, Percy, I want you to meet Earl Hove,' and hurries away to attend to his other guests. There is a brief interval during which the two agree that this is the rottenest party they were ever at and possibly exchange a remark or two about the weather, then the Earl of Brighton speaks:

'I didn't quite get the name. Earl of Hove, did he say?'

'No, just Earl Hove.'

My lord of Brighton blinks as if he had been struck between the eyes with a wet fish. A coldness creeps into his manner.

'You mean *plain* Earl Hove?'

'That's right.'

'No "of"?'

'No, no "of."'

'Good God!'

There is a tense silence. You can see the Earl of Brighton's lip curling.

'Ah, well,' he says at length, 'it takes all sorts to make a world, does it not?' and Earl Hove slinks off with his ears pinned back and drinks far too many sherries in the hope of restoring his self-respect. Practically all the Earls who are thrown sobbing out of cocktail parties are non-ofs. They can't take it, poor devils.

I don't think I have much more to say on this subject, though I know you would gladly have me ramble on for ever. I will merely add that in certain parts of America – notably Brooklyn – if the resident wishes to attract the attention of a visiting Earl he shouts 'Hey, Oil!'

June 1954

Alan Coren

FROM THE DIARY OF SAMUEL PEPYS JNR.

AUGUST

20. Up betimes, and some unsettlynge grutchings of pain in the Great Bowel, I praye God not the Sicknesse but meerly a Winde arising from my having fasted for so long. I truste that this new Executone Bjorn Borg Grape 'n' Clam Diet is not too austere at onlie three hundred calories *per diem*, already I find myselfe unable to jogge as heretofore, being too weery to zippe up my trackesuite.

Downstayres, to where my dear children are at break-faste in our elegant nooke and my son Samuel III much agitated at my

'Jolly nice of the Duke to retain poor old Jenkins after his awful wounding at Inkerman.'

pallor, admonishing mee earnestly not to drive to my office. His concerne touches mee deeplie, but it is shortlie out that he fears that, should I indeed have contrackted the Sicknesse, I wil contaminate the Mercedes which he has bespoke this nighte for a heavy date and does not wish for himselfe or his beloved that they catch buboes from the upholsterie. My younger daughter enraged at this; she and I were ever moste close, and teers sprynge to her fair eyes at the thoughte of my Deth, since she fears that I do not carrye enough insurance to see her through college.

Yet further dischorde thereat attends, however, my elder daughter declayming the opinion that shee has the prioritie distrainte, since while it is possible to work one's way through college, it is not possible to work one's way through analysis; it is presentlye runninge out at around five hundred per session and there are many yeers ahead, they have not yet even reached the poynte at which she muste recognyze her pathological hatred of her father and rejecte himme.

I turne thereat to my deer wyfe who is wobblynge upon the electrical exerciser, to supplicate her tenderest intervention in these matters touchynge upon our familie; but shee lets out such a shriek at my elder daughter for darynge to place her sanity above her mother's need for a new buste and bobbed nose, five thousand minimum, thatte I creepe from the house in despayre.

21. Up early, and downe to meet with Doctor Schumacher at his office, my Guttes being no better though no Lumpes, thanke God, appearyng; some Ague of the joyntes, but doubtless due to my deer wyfe takynge the circumspect precaution of lettynge me sleepe in the yarde.

I am met by Doctor Schumacher's nurse-person, a goodlie buxome soul who takes my hat and coate wyth rubber gloves and throwes them in the trash, and bids me enter the surgerie. Wythin minutes, the Doctor appeares upon the closed circuit screene above my head, explayninge that there is much Sicknesse about in the City and hee is therefore takynge his surgerie from his jacuzzi in Palm Springs, and solicitously enquires of mee what might be the trouble?

I descrybe my distressing symptoms to him, and he listens most carefully, noddynge from tyme to tyme. When I have finished, I aske him what he thinkes it might be, and he replyes that he thinkes it might by anything from five hundred to a thousand, dependynge upon whether I require a second visit. I tell him that I praye it is not the Plague, and hee is very sympathetic, reminding mee that if it is Plague it would mean puttynge the house on the market and talkynge to his brother Sam atte the Schumacher Finance & Loan. Hee would, since I was an olde and deere friend as well as a patient, put in a good word with his brother, but his advyce to mee was that if I was pulling downe less than a hundred thousand a yeare, I would be extreamely unwise even to thinke about contrackting the Plague. If I did catche it, *nolens volens*, his professional opinion was that I shoulde cutte my losses, and die.

To my office later, and much excitement! No less than three Executive Vice-Presidents have swoll'd up in the nighte, and there is much eeger jockeyinge for their positions. This hath thrown us all into a great whirl, and if th'Almighty spares mee yet strikes down Kowalski and Rappaport, I could yette emerge from the Sicknesse as Senior Head of Sales Conceptualisation (South).

Home at my most fleete to impart the news to my deere wyfe, but she away at her yoghurt class, and the lockes all changed. I can see my deere children, through the windowes, but they shreeke at me to take myselfe to a goodlie distance.

22. Up at dawne shakynge with a Palsie and dredfull red weals upon my backe; but these, I thinke, due not to the Sicknesse but to

my sleepynge on the rail-roade trackes. Rose betimes, and hobbled to the barber, my razor being at home; a fyne discourse with the learned man, hee being of the opinion that the Plague is due to the blackamoors and will be cured only upon the application of shotgunnes; since I grow exceedynge uneasy at talke of the Sicknesse, I turn the topicke to the Recession, and fynde the man eeger of economicke solution: since the Recession can onlie be due to the blackamoors, shotgunnes are the one sure answer. Wee are keenlie discussing the twinne matters of Communism and Homosexualitie, the honeste barber holding that these are being spread daily throughout the realm by the blackamoors, when there is a great tumulte above our heads from the television screen, announcynge thatte a fortunate houseperson from the fayre city of Boise, Idaho, has just won ten thousand dollars on *Guess My Bubo!*, the newest game showe, upon which contestants suff'ring all manner of noxious infections – quinsy, thrush, stone, head-

'Just think, my dear . . . if this is what man is capable of achieving in the seventeenth century, imagine what he'll be capable of by the twentieth!'

mould, pox, dropsie, convulsions, wormes, imposthume, scurvy – pass before a jurie of their peeres, who have to discover the *genuine* sufferer of the Plague: should hee deceive them all, hee receives not onlie ten thousand dollars, but also cosmetick embalmynge to resemble the movie star of his or her choyce, a genuine mahoganette coffin with near-brass handels, and free cleansing of his premises, after his interment, by a top-name fumigator!

Truly, God Almighty smiles upon this His countrie!

From the barber, much cheered in spirit, but founde increasing traffic in the streetes of drear processions of mourners as the Sicknesse takes holde; this so distressed me, I turned into a hostelry, despyte the rigors of my diet, in search of a revyvinge cordial, styrred not shaken. The concoction not entirely to my lykinge, I enquired of its maker as to the whereaboutes of the regular barman; and was forwyth informed that he had juste that morning make a killynge upon the Stock Market and retired to the Bahamas.

Apparently, upon the very fyrste winde of the Plague, he had gone heavily into Funeral Parlour stock.

25. Up betimes, the 6.40 Rock Island freight having made an unconscionable noise a-shuntynge, and telephoned my deere wyfe; an unknown man answeringe, I was greatly puzzled, the hour being so early, whereat my deere wyfe came upon the line to informe me that my elder daughter havynge persuaded her, after deepe and meaningfull discussions with her analyst, that the collapse of Western Civilization was entyrely due to the destructive infibulations of the one-to-one relationshyppe, she had therefore seized upon the fortuitous opportunitie presented by the Plague to replace me with Clyde, a major garbage operative. I immediately replyed that I had it on the very best authoritie that the collapse of Western Civilization was, in facte, entirely due to blackamoors; at which my deere wyfe enquired whether I should care to come round and saye that to Clyde's face.

Not wishing to avayle myselfe of this dubious offer, I repaired instead, through the increasingly emptie streetes, to what is now my regular hostelrie; I fynde that by dropping a grape into my dry martini, I am enabled both to satisfy my dietry strictures and simultaneously to alleviate my wretchednesse. Though it was yet but seven o'clock, the place was full of unshaven men in three-piece suits: upon enquirie, I ascertained that these were lawyers who had spent the whole of the previous night celebrating a major landmarke, nay, a very watershedde, in the historie of human litigation!

It transpyred that the next-of-kin of a woman dead of the Plague in Redwing, Minnesota, had successfully sued the owner of the barn in which expert evidence had established that the offendynge rat had been born and bred, for one hundred million dollars, the attorney being in for thirtie per cent of the grosse. With upwardes of six thousand soules now perishing daily in California alone, is it any wonder that the lawyers were dancing upon the tables?

26. To my office early, all now assured that I am sufferynge but a Colicke, but no great joye to be gleaned: Kowalski and Rappaport in seeming great healthe, and, yet more grave, my own sales area grievously dwindled through the Sicknesse. Commissions may be well downe this quarter.

However, much brightened by a Presidential broadcast at noon, our beloved Leader appearing hale and lumplesse, his trousers tucked into his bootes after a fashion now recognized as one of the greatest decisions of his career. His horse also in evident high spirits. Briefly, his message is that, with some thirty millions now neatly dead, the unemployment dilemma has vanished at a stroke; further, given the unhealthy proximity in which the inhabitants had chosen to live, the ghetto problem was now a thynge of the paste. At longe laste, The Shinynge City was in view! Certainly, I cannot have been alone in noting yet another new twinkle in his already sparkling eye, and it may well be that the Rumours concerning the *fons et origo* of the Sicknesse may not be as unfounded as I first conceived them to be. No doubt, in the fulnesse of tyme, credit will emerge where it is due; certain it is, the Plague hath been good for Businesse, and I should not bee the fyrste to remark that the businesse of America is Businesse!

Of course, the matter must not be allowed to get out of hande; as our great Leader took paynes to enunciate, enough was enough, and a method should now be soughte of eradicating the Plague swiftlie, much as had been achieved during its successful visitation of my namesake's London, with a purgative conflagration. Sufferers should be quietly removed to prevent further spreading of the Sicknesse. To that ende, he had discharged his trustie colleague, Mr Caspar Weinberger, with the dutie of discovering some device which could be counted upon to destroye people, while leaving property intact.

August 1981

'Here's the bastard now **and** he's carrying our Maude's bladder.'

'RUINED, ALBERT? AND SHALL WE HAVE TO LEAVE OUR LITTLE NEST?'

5

BLESS THEM!

'We were relieved to find a school that wasn't soft on uniforms.'

Geoffrey Willans

MOLESWORTH THE GOOD

Contains: Time-Tables of hols, girls, rats, farms and good conduc.

Dec. 29. Down to stay at aunt ciss farm for rest of hols chiz. Aunt ciss meet us in britches also weedy girl called ermintrude and avakuee called Ivy. Who is a titch. They sa where is your brother. I sa i do not kno honest injun but he was here a minit ago and they find him in lugage rack blubbing. molesworth 11 sa I haf pute him there. He is a sneke and just because he coming to school nex term he swanks and mucks about. He is absolutely weedy.

Dec. 30. All girls are weedy, espeshally ermintrude.

Dec. 31. There is a tuough bull here called Jack it is ferce and I tie bunch of carrots to its tale. Molesworth 11 sa go it and then snekes to aunt Ciss chiz and she sa sit quietly with ermintrude chiz chiz chiz. Ermintrude is goody goody she loves pritty flowers and doesnt muck about with her food. She sa it is rude to make lake in mashed potatoes with gravy. She likes prunes (swank). Tonite Aunt ciss read us a book eric or little by little which is not bad actually. Ermintrude sa why can't you be good like that.

Jan. 1. New Year resoution detmin to be GOOD.

Jan. 2. Try out my catterpult and see Aunt Ciss in her britches. Refrane. Then molesworth 11 come up and sa 'you haf a face like a squashed tomatoe.' when i do not tuough him up he sa it like a trillion squashed tomatoes. At tea I wash hands and some of face.

Ermintrude sa i look more human. Chiz? She is not bad actually. She haf not missed sunda school for 3 years. Coo.

Jan. 3. Aunt ciss give us party and we pla postmans knock chiz chiz chiz weedy. I call out little girl with pink ribon but when she see me she blub and run away. molesworth 11 go out but when he do not call anebody aunt ciss find him in the larder eating jelly. He tie ermintrude's pigtale to xmas tree and get sent to bed. Absolute snubs. I hide under sofa to avoid dancing actually and find ivy there. I sit on her tofees but she sa garn she like them better with hairs on.

Jan. 4. Find topping dead rat in one of the lofts and molesworth 11 sa I can give him two sloshes for it. no i sa you can haf it for nothing. He sa thanks awfully then call me measly flea and rune away. Gratitude? at nite I find rat in bed and rise full of wrath to slorter him but rember i am good. All the same will tuough him up when I stop. Put rat tidily in washbasin but friten maid in morning when she come and she haf hystericks. Aunt Ciss give me 6 with hairbrush chiz. Ermintrude ignore me.

Jan. 7. Ermintrude is peculiar she do lessons in the hols for fun and dances weedily. She give me her autograff book as favour were everyone had written weedy things like cheerio gwen. I draw fat person aunt Ciss but change it into cow. Ermintrude get batey and sa she will not let me see her botany Book now. She praktise piano fairy dance awful. I sa not bad and she call me Sir galahad. unfortunately Molesworth 11 hapned to be by on way to larder and he larff like anything. He is weedy and swanks just becos he haf septick spots.

Jan. 11. Aunt ciss take us to panto in her old grid. jack and the beanstalk rather weedy as they all fall in love. molesworth 11 flick toofee papers on peoply downstairs and Ivy eat orange. molesworth 11 buy pips for a d. and bombs downstairs like anything. Aunt ciss give him 6d for hitting mrs fulkington-

Brown. Ermintrude aloof but she sa the faires are beautiful: widow Twanky say dam and ivy larff so much she choke and swallow pip.

Jan. 12. Snow. Detmin to STOP being good.

Jan. 13. Toda i will tuough up the bull, hide aunt ciss britches snoball ermintrude and teach molesworth 11 sharp lesson. Go out mightily to carry out plans ree bull. and coolect coollossal snoball but bull turn and lick my hand and i haf not the heart. It is not a bad bull so detmin to throw snoball at molesworth 11 insted. Find him coolecting bad words from bill the labourer in harnes room. Wam bonk throw ball but hit bill. Molesworth 11 learn new words. Ivy come in highly delighted she haf lost her pants but ermintrude practise greek dance indoors. I think she is mouldy after all.

Jan. 15. Moan groan can't seem to stop being good. Must do better. Ermintrude come into sno but pla girly games. She sa eenee meenee miny mo and wallflowers wallflowers grow so tall but ermintrude is the strongest and out you must go. molesworth 11 pla but chizzes and so he haf not been tagged. Ermintrude sa sliding is comon but skating graceful. She swank she can skate so we find pond with thin ice and she fall in splosh. Aunt Ciss sa what a shame then give us sixpence. She is sporting.

Jan. 17. Molesworth 11 teech bills words to the parot but parot tell him off. Parot is Chapel.

Jan. 20. Rover the sheepdog dig up rat so

'Very commendable, Bestwick. I didn't think you'd be able to give up smoking and drinking for Lent.'

i prepare trap for molesworth 11, pute it in his bed also holly and buket of water on door. Then I sa fetch the air gune molesworth 11 o you might and he go off but meet ermintrude who sa she always happy to rune an erand. Molesworth 11 sa okay and while he gone he steal her butter rashon. Water fall on ermintrude and she sa I am a beastly beast and she will never let me see her botany Book. Don't want to so boo. molesworth 11 discover rat and offer it to parrot. Parrot use one of bill's words and ivy come back wet as she haf sat down in pudle. All sent to bed.

Jan. 24. Back to school weedy school. Moan and jasper. Packing and all sad even bull and parrot. Bull roars and i give it old carrot but Ivy blub becos it was hers. Parrot sing Polly pute the ketle on which it only do under stress of great emotion. Sa goodby and off to station in old grid. Molesworth 11 sa he will take photo of ermintrude but when he click camera out fly rat on spring. Train comes in express called corfe Castle 4–6–2 streamlined. chuff chuff wizz wave to aunt ciss and put molesworth 11 in lugage rack. Settle down to micky mouse weekly. Boo to school.

Jan. 25. 7267354 secs to end of term.
THE END.

February 1940

John Betjeman

A FRANK ADDRESS TO THE OLD SCHOOL

My dear boys, it was kind and wise of your Headmaster to choose me to address you. Just when I was reaching the port stage of my excellent dinner with him last night, you were supposed to be dropping off to sleep in your dormitories and those of you who had not strings fastened to your toes to wake you if you snored, or who were not suspended by your feet from the rafters for not being good enough at football, were no doubt trying to get some rest.

I like an early cup of tea in the morning, and at seven, when mine was brought, the well-known sound of the bell woke you from dreams of home to the more familiar whitewashed walls of school, the rows of iron bedsteads, each bed with its pale burden under the red blankets. I think there must be some educational supply company which has a monopoly of school bells. Their note is always the same, not so irritating as the telephone, but more terrifying; not so mellow as the church bell, but more ominous; not so evocative of excitement as a fire alarm, but conveying the relentless monotony to which it calls you.

As I lay in bed wondering what I was going to say to you, I heard your merry little feet pattering over cool linoleum to some healthy cold tubs to freshen you up for the day's work. It was raining hard outside and I was imagining that you would soon have to be hurrying away from a hasty breakfast, across wet courts and under windy arches to classrooms smelling of ink, old boots, old biscuits and bat oil, there to bluff your way through the morning, trying to prevent your form master finding out that you had not done last night's preparation. By this time my breakfast was brought to me in bed on a tray, grapefruit, eggs and bacon, toast, coffee, marmalade, and *no porridge whatsoever.*

Do not imagine, however, I am trying to make you envious. I have got up after a nice hot bath and at a reasonable hour and can see things clearly. You will only be able to have these privileges by becoming so ill that you have to be moved to the sanatorium. But even then you will get well again and it will be doubly hard to adjust yourselves to the rigours of the school curriculum.

And, dear boys, let me remind you of the date. We are early in October. Christmas is a long way off. The Christmas holidays are short; then comes that terrible term when it is so cold that you have chilblains on your toes as well as on your fingers. Then there are even shorter holidays at Easter and after that the long, long summer term with its unspeakably boring hours of grilling cricket followed by the dangers and the duckings of the bathing place.

But I am anticipating. I wonder how many of you will survive unscathed until the summer term? Looking round at this sea of faces, I wonder how many of you will be expelled; how many times each of you will be beaten by the prefects for leaving your clothes about, by your housemasters for not doing enough work, by the Headmaster for more serious crimes. Some of you I see already have spots. During the term, owing to the difference in the food from what you are accustomed to at home, these spots will grow angrier and boils will appear on the backs of your necks. But these are not complaints bad enough to earn you a rest in the sanatorium.

Well, it is time for me to go now. Your Headmaster has kindly put his car at my disposal to take me to the airport. I am taking a 'plane to a diplomatic mission in Bermuda. Besides having ample private means, I am paid by the Minister of Commonwealth Relations, for whom I am a sort of roving ambassador, at £5,000 a year with hotel bills and expenses extra. I shall stay at the best place in whatever is the capital of Bermuda, and I shall be away for some months as my work is of national, nay global, significance. Perhaps your Headmaster would like me to talk to you again next summer and if I have the time I will come. But I am a busy man.

October 1953

'I WONDER IF THERE'S A REALLY *NICE* LITTLE BOY IN THE ROOM WHO WOULD LIKE TO RUN UPSTAIRS AND LOOK FOR MUMMY'S SPECTACLES!'

He. 'WHERE DO ANIMALS GO WHEN THEY DIE?'
She. 'ALL GOOD ANIMALS GO TO HEAVEN, BUT THE BAD ONES GO TO THE NATURAL HISTORY MUSEUM.'

'And another thing – you'll have to
stop him drawing all over the walls.'

'You probably don't remember me – I
was always in bed by the time
you got home.'

The Child-hater

6

THE ENGLISH ABROAD

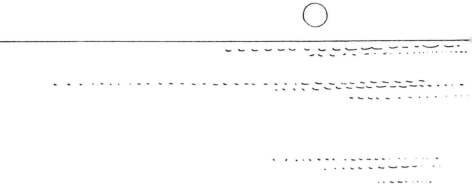

'Isn't it that awful couple we met on the boat?'

Alex Atkinson

HAVE MONOCLE – WILL TRAVEL

(*Miss Vicki Benet, an American TV star, is reported to be offering a contract of a thousand dollars a week to any suitable British peer who will go to California to appear on television.*)

Dear Miss Benet, – I beg to apply for the post of televison Peer which I understand you have vacant.

I am a Lord. I and my whole family have been at one time or another connected with show business, an ancestor of mine having received a title for arranging an intro for the King with Nell Gwyn in an old-world alley off Drury Lane, London, and my grandfather having in his younger days been highly thought of by a Miss Prissy Beaufort, a chorus lady, who was to have been my grandmother but who subsequently eloped with a Spanish nobleman, taking the watch which was to have been mine at age twenty-one. I also once had the honour to be presented to Mr Terry-Thomas. So you see the smell of grease-paint is no stranger to me, to say nothing of narrowly missing being given an audition for the famous Greek drama, *The Frogs*, written specially for the nobility by William Wallace. I had a bad cold at the time, but am proud to say was on the short list for programme sellers and went backstage to see the flowers. I am sure I could arrange a glimpse of Royalty for you at the next show, as I am in touch with Mr Rex North and other influential personalities.

You need have no fear of getting me past the Customs in America, as my family have been Tory for generations, the family motto being in Latin, the translation being 'Elephants, wishing to cross a stream, always send the weakest first.' I am a staunch supporter of freedom, Mr McCarthy, and racial discrimination, and my present job is connected with the selling of motor cars. I also have an interest, on my mother's side, in a small night-club.

I have not, as yet, actually appeared on television, as the custom in this country is to concentrate on Ladies instead of Lords. This is only common politeness after all, and one cannot grudge it them as cold cream adverts seem to have died out. I am, however, something of an entertainer. I am enclosing a cutting from the *Evening Standard*, where it tells all about me doing my conjuring with solid silver egg cups at a Mayfair party at which many models were present. (I do not wish to seem to boast, but I am on speaking terms with several models, and one jockey.) Also sometimes in the House of Lords (where I often spend an afternoon) I have gained much laughter at my witty sallies on various topics of interest. It has been said that I could rival Lord Mancroft with practice.

I have watched television many times at my employer's house, and believe it has a great future, as on the television you can see the people, where on the wireless you can't, you can only hear them.

My age is forty-one, and I was, of course, at Harrow, as was Sir Winston, who is related to the Duke of Marlborough. Many have said I look no more than thirty-seven, although I do not wear my body-belt. My hair is going thin on top, but I have a small whig which my father used to wear at Eton-Harrow matches which would do nicely for younger parts. I am adept at putting it on so that nobody would know.

I am not married as yet, as I have always been interested in horses, but I assure you I and my family have no old-fashioned prejudices against marrying into money. I am sure by your photo I would get on well together with you and that our association would be to our mutual benefit.

I enclose a recent photo taken at Brighton with a young lady I know slightly who is going to be a model (bust 37, hips 36, blonde hair), also one at Ascot last year where I am in full costume. I assume one can hire these costumes in California too, and think it would be very suitable for ordinary parts. My peer's robes are somewhat big for me, but would be all right for doing the commercials in. I hope I would not have to eat many corn flakes, as they are inclined to disagree.

My wardrobe also includes blazer, cricket togs, dinner jacket (made specially for me), fishing-hat, hacking-jacket, waders, Guards tie and an A.R.P. uniform dyed green, from when we stood alone. My great-aunt, the Marchioness of Lum, whose husband was a game-warden in Fifeshire for his health, has promised me a small kilt if my application is successful if I promise not to stain it.

I have, of course, a slight lisp to prove I am authentic. I would naturally have to give a fortnight's notice, but am otherwise ready to take up my new duties at once. Perhaps you would be kind enough to state briefly the climate of California, as I have to be careful about my vests. Whilst writing, I would also like to mention that my mother is an excellent cook and has some very old English antique furniture. I could easily persuade her to give it away for practically a song if she thought it would be going to a good home. I don't know if you know anyone in California in need of a cook. My sister, the Hon. Adelaide, who came out five years ago, also asks me to state that she has a strong controlto voice and is taking tap and modern ballroom including South American. Her teeth are much straighter now.

Please return photos, especially the one at Brighton, as it must not fall into the wrong hands.

I remain,
Your humble servant,
CAMCHESTER (GEORGE)

p.s. – Do not consider Lord Woolton, who is sure to apply. Between ourselves, he was in trade.

July 1955

Brigid Keenan

BLUBBINGS OF A MEMSAHIB

I am honestly the last person who should have become an expatriate wife. Apart from my claustrophobia, vertigo, insecurity, indecisiveness and general emotional haemophilia, I am fearful of everything, from being alone, to British High Commissioners, to flying and lifts. (I suppose I inherit all this from my mother who is known as Doomwatch in the family. When I asked her long ago why she invariably expected the worst to happen she said that in her experience it always had.)

I used to tell myself that it is not possible to die of rabies *and* be killed in a plane crash *and* crushed to death in an audience stampede in the Indira Gandhi stadium while watching the Russian circus *and* be struck by lightning *and* beheaded by the ceiling fan when it flies off its mooring, but I've learned one thing in India which is that with reincarnation one could have all those grisly ends – and more – it would just be over a longer span of time.

And then there is the small matter of my career. Before I married I was a fashion writer, even a women's editor. In fact, I was once described as a *Young Meteor*. But you can't be any of those things in a dusty suburb of New Delhi where I now live attached to an economist involved in development aid, so the Young Meteor has become a fallen star, or perhaps satellite would be a kinder description.

In our last posting in the West Indies I wrote a book about Kashmir – it took years and years and cost a fortune in stamps because all the research had to be done by post to London or Delhi. The week I finished it my husband came home from the office and announced that we were being transferred – to Delhi. I think the sound that came from my throat at this news is known as a primal scream. (You would not exactly risk being crushed to death in the stampede to publish my book, but I live in hope.) Sometimes at dinner parties I confide in my neighbours that I was once a fashion editor and then I see a flicker of disbelief in their eyes and I wish I hadn't.

The most humiliating instance of this sort happened in the West Indies when I went to look at the clothes in a trendy boutique. The designer herself happened to be in the shop, so, plucking up my courage I went and introduced myself to her – 'I'm *so* interested in your collection blah blah, you see I used to be Fashion Editor of *The Sunday Times* blah blah ...' The designer looked me up and down coldly as though I was a bag lady who'd got in by mistake, so I lowered my eyes in embarrassment and then – horrors – I caught sight of my hem – I'd got my dress on inside out and it was home-made and all the seams were frayed with long, tangled threads hanging from them.

In India, I am quite scared of our servants, but not as much as I used to be, and not as badly as the young ex-pat who was so terrified of his cook that he used to introduce his guests to him, 'Ram Lal, I don't believe you've met Professor Theobalds and Sir Nigel Parkes ...' My own worst servant moment comes on Monday mornings when Harry, the cook, appears at my side at the breakfast table with his Book. In this, I am supposed to write down what I'd like him to make for the week's meals. 'Harry,' I say decisively, 'on Monday we will have maca-

'You get used to the English Quarter.'

roni cheese with tomato salad.' Then I remember that he is supposed to be working his way through Madhur Jaffrey because he doesn't know many Indian dishes, so I say, 'No, sorry, not macaroni cheese. Try the Moghlai Chicken Braised with Almonds and Raisins on page 39 of the Indian cook book.' Then I remember that our daughter will be eating with us and that she can't stand chilli-hot food, so I say, 'No Harry, we will have sausages and chips.' Then I remember that we are out of English sausages and we can't have the local ones for fear of pork brain worm, and so I desperately fall back on the macaroni cheese again.

My husband and I eat extremely fast. This has never reared its head as a problem in

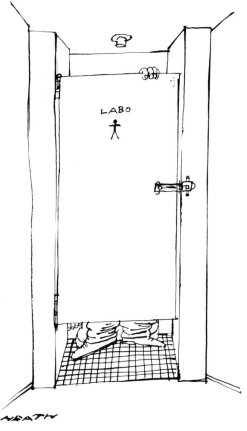

ENJOYING LOCAL DISHES

England but here it's really embarrassing. At 8 p.m. the two of us sit down – rather self-consciously – to be served our dinner and at three and a half minutes past we've finished. There's barely time for Harry and Paul to make it back to the kitchen before they must dash in again to clear away. (Paul, by the way, is Harry's son and our bearer, and the living spit of Manuel in *Fawlty Towers*.)

After the Monday morning scene with the Book, I move into the garden to discuss the estate with the *mali* (gardener). We live in a little suburban house in a road called Poorvi Marg, which turns out to mean East End (we are Delhi's East Enders – I wonder if our neighbours complain about the ghastly smell of European food). It is on the flight path to the airport, opposite a low-cost housing estate for thousands and near some quarries, so that aside from the general Indian hubbub outside, there is the scream of aircraft and the earth-shaking boom of the quarry going up every now and then. (When my husband is away I can work myself into believing that the explosions are some sort of uprising – a new mutiny – and I can't be alone in thinking this, for some of the Embassies have installed strong rooms in their peoples' houses in which they are supposed to lock themselves with walkie-talkie sets should rioting mobs start howling at the gates.)

Anyway, our garden is about 25 ft by 25 ft but it is an oasis in the dust and we take it very seriously. When I first came here the *mali* told me that he would have some celery ready at the end of the month. I was hugely impressed that he could grow it in only ten days but presumed this was some mysterious thing to do with the Indian climate, so I enthused about how much we liked fresh vegetables and how pleased I was that he was growing some, etc, etc, while he looked more and more confused. Eventually it turned out that he had been asking for his salary at the end of the month.

Things like this are always happening in

India – and you have to be careful when giving instructions not to leave anything unsaid such as please don't boil the lettuce before you make the salad.

Our gate is like a safety curtain between us and the 800 million Indians outside. Kashmiri carpet salesmen and lace vendors and snake-charmers and men offering camel-rides are constantly trying to penetrate it without much success, but not long after the celery business a woman appeared holding out an empty bowl. 'We cannot turn away any person asking for food,' I announced with my Mother Theresa face on, and asked Harry to find something to fill her bowl. He reappeared with a saucepan of *dal* but to my amazement the woman was furious. It turned out that she was *selling the bowl* and the last thing she wanted was to have it all messed up with food.

We came to India a year ago last October. It was the middle of the night when we arrived, tired and disorientated and nervous about our New Life. No one turned up to meet us at the airport, and though we tried to put on brave faces for the children – 'Aaaah, the exotic smell of India,' 'Girls, look at those pretty ladies in saris,' etc –

THE BRITISH CHARACTER
ADAPTABILITY TO FOREIGN CONDITIONS.

when our younger daughter burst into tears and said she wanted to go home with the nice British Airways' hostess, it was exactly what we were all feeling.

We stayed in a hotel called Claridges (no relation) for two months while we looked for a house. I cried a lot in Claridges, but I cried even more when we left the womb of our room there, for then we were on our own in the sub-continent having to cope with the endless problems of electricity, water, air conditioners and telephone. Which reminds me, our telephone has been terminally ill for some time and yesterday I made the fatal mistake of reporting it out of order. Since then a telephone engineer has rung every ten minutes and shouted at me in Hindi before hanging up.

Often I wonder what on earth this is all about. Sometimes I think that we ex-pat wives are merely measuring out our lives with coffee spoons, simply passing time before we move on somewhere else. But sometimes I think I am luckier than anyone I know because it's not coffee spoons but soup-ladles of life that are being offered to me. There are moments – especially when looking at the grandiose buildings of Lutyens' New Delhi through the evening dust haze, or wandering, unthreatened, in the dense streets of the bazaar in Old Delhi, or enjoying the brilliant beauty of the Rajasthani women who work on the roads and on building sites – when I am ecstatic, euphoric, about India. But there are other moments when the whole Indian experience shrinks down to the discomfort of having to clean my sensitive teeth with ice-cold drinking water from a bottle.

Must remember to get someone to bring out some Sensodyne.

January 1988

Michael Bywater

PARADISE MISLAID

The British Ecological Society has announced 23 expedition awards, all to parties organised by young would-be explorers. The Guardian

June 2nd 198–

Well here we are up the old Matto Grosso. Who wuold of thought the Fojrds of Finland wuold be like this? Never in my darkest, dreams did I ~~invs enivsa invasadge~~ got a clue about the snakes and stuff, let alone the tree's, which it must be siad are well amazing. The place is crawling with coon's but Mr Hanky say's as we mus'tnt notice nor say nothink in case of offending Wellington and Florizel, thuogh niether of them give a ~~fu bugg~~ dam, matter of fact Wellington says they a lower form of life, for a ethi enthic coon he is a real snob.

The major indusry of this place is rain. My bog-roll is totally swolled up. And somtheing is moving about inside my Walkman, I can hear its little footstep's. Maybe its a native ho ho ho they are graet at Limbo dancing, a Walkman wuold be no problem. I just told this joke to Florizel an he puncht me in the, muoth.

Plenty of tree's and stuff but Hanky wo'nt say what they are, jus says 'You are here to appreciate and assimilate, taxomony is a repressive dicsipline of the middle clases.' We havne't seen any aminals yet niether.

June 3rd 198–

We still havne't seen any but the jugnle is

ovbiously full of ~~esco coxit~~ queer and strange animals with loud voices, one of them has eat my DM's in the nihgt. I got up and put my foot in and this thing ran out the toecap, it was greenish, in one night it done what four year's up the Shed fail to ~~achie~~ do, e.g. ruin them. That is £32.50 down the drian or rather down the throat!! Hanky say's this wil give us a insight into the problems of alternative society~~'s. No wonder we all call him 'Wank~~ You can gues what we call him an no wonder, what a ~~cu~~ fool.

One of these day's, ~~vegnean veangan vengac~~ we will push his teeth in.

June 4th 198–

This morning saw a bit of a ~~contrm contrepe~~ punch-up on account of ~~W~~ Hanky giving out a stupid book called 'Lord of the Flie's', he tried to make us read it but natch it all swole up in the rain just like my bog-roll and Florizel says 'Hey, colonialist oppressive ~~shi~~ junk, man!', his father is in the Education Sub Comitte and ~~Wa~~ Hanky is shi dead scared of him even though here we are, billions of miles away in the jugnles of, I think we decided it was Switzerland.

June 5th 198–

We are defnitely in Tasmania. There are Brazil nuts everywhere. The qeustion is, where do we go from here? We got a whole lot of map's but no compass, at least we got a compass but Eric drunk the ~~aclo alhole~~ booze out of it and it just flops over now, juts like Eric ha ha ha. ~~Wa~~ Hanky say 'Wait for nihgtfall and we will nagivate by means of the star's, a anceint trick discovered by the Sumerian's', then Florizel give him this mean Look and Hanky think (Oh ~~fu~~ dear) and say's 'Of course the ~~coo~~ Blakcs new of it first, they jus't didnt chose to go anywhere althouhg they cuold if theyd of wante'd to'.

Later

Well nihgt has fallen and we had this decromatic vote on what was the North Pole, it turn out to be prety interesting. Hanky come out of his tent looking red and hot with Snakehips O'Brien (Social Studeis & Communinty Projecs) doing up her zip, 'We been looking up stuff in the Anostromy book' according to Hanky but we cuold see what been going on, if he think's we were born yesterday, we we'rent. Then Hanky say 'Civilization is north-wetsward, chaps!' which dosent go down to well with geuss who, Florizel!!!, who says 'Hey man, you fascist dictator or what?, also racist cultural suprecamist!' and Hanky says 'Why?' and Florizel says 'You ovbiously been ~~sha scr~~ having a go on Snakehips excluding the Black Man from his cultural heritage, white trash', and Snakehips look hard at Florizel, stand there in his Laurence Corner fatigeus and gunbelt with his banana wrap round his head like a real mercenary and next thing, Snakehips in the tent with Florizel and Hanky standing there looking like a stick of cerely.

June 6th 198–

Stil dark and stil walking, Hanky nagging us from the front. Every time anyone say 'When ~~the f~~ we going to get there?' all Hanky say is 'Do not be so goal directed, this is not a gramer school, we are helping yuo to find yuor true selves ecncountering ethnic civilsations without prejudice, throw away yuor cultural bagage.' I said 'All my bagage got is (a) pink bog roll swole up; (2) copy of Lord of the Fleis, all swole up, and (d) Weetabix, all swole up.' Hanky did'nt luagh, just say nonsense, i.e. 'The important thing is to keep your course fixed against a distant refrence point or else you go round in circels'. We have just passed a Tree for the third time.

June 7th 198–

At las we know where we are! We are in Borneo! We met some blokes, they invite us to a Party, I do not know abuot local ethinc customs and absorbing fauna and the diversity of man, e.g. what Hanky was on abuot, but they kno how to give a party, we all got really ~~pi~~ drunk and the coo locals were real freindly, going around sqeuzing our arms an such. At first we were dead woried on account of cabinals but Hanky said, 'Do not push yuor luck, keep yuor gutter fascism to yuorselves, these people have a cultural heritage as rich as yuors althuogh diferntly expresed.' This speech gone down A.1. and the ~~wo~~ locals luagh a lot took Hanky off to some special private party. Weetabix now green and furry but so what? Thei'rs this great smell of cooking and wer'e looking forward to a decent meal, our first for day's.

April 1987

'NO, MADAM, A PASSPORT IS NOT NECESSARY FOR SCOTLAND.'

David Hunt

THE GRAND OBJECT OF TRAVELLING

No prizes are offered for knowing that what Dr Johnson called the grand object of travelling was 'to see the shores of the Mediterranean.' In summer, millions of his countrymen take him literally. They make for the shores and stick to them, the adhesive being a blend of oil and suntan cream. When I try and form a mental picture of a half-naked Johnson on the beach at Benidorm or Limassol the image does not come readily at call; but he was a great traveller and it might be worth conjecturing how he would plan a visit to the modern Mediterranean. After all, his contemporaries found it thoroughly diverting that he should have toured the Western Islands and that was an effort far more remarkable and toilsome in his time than even more distant journeys today. We know his tastes well enough; let us consider how they could be catered for by a package tour, and what advice could be given him.

He had an affection for islands, and here he would find a wider selection than in the Hebrides. They come in two main varieties, large and small. Each has its own special merits. Sicily, Crete or Cyprus give you enough room to spread. In all of them you can have as much variety as you like, from bathing beaches to Greek temples. Besides, the natives are so friendly and so very pro-British. The wine is drinkable and the summer weather reliable though the steady north wind that thunders down on Crete does become a little monotonous after a while.

For my part, deserting Johnson, I have a liking for small islands, especially Greek ones. It is a well-shared taste. George Orwell's road from Wigan Pier has long ago deserted Blackpool and now leads more readily to the Eastern Mediterranean; even the Euxine at last deserves its name since the charter plane has revealed its Golden Beaches. Rhodes has become a suburb of Stockholm. Cos is known for more than its lettuces. Try Mytilene for a change. Lord Charlemont, a friend of Johnson's, was there in 1749, as his youthful diaries, just published for the first time, have revealed. He was shocked to discover that 'the women seem to have arrogated to themselves the department and privileges of the men.' (He also recorded some remarks about Sappho which in his old age he obliterated so thoroughly that they are lost for ever.) The Lesbian women have retained a reputation for ferocity; in 1945 I remember a women's demonstration against the Sub-Prefect which ended in several of them biting him most severely.

I know a small island off Chios where the beaches and the sea are as clean and as translucent as they were fifty years ago when I first visited it. I am not afraid to mention it because it has no hotel and the traveller must follow the advice given him by Carl Baedeker in 1908: not to rely on the local inns or khans but on being hospitably received by 'the respectable natives'. (He also advised him to wear a suit of grey tweed and to carry stones to throw at the dogs.) Very hospitable the inhabitants are, too, both there and in London, where they spend their working lives in the shipping business. I might also put in a word for Montecristo but as most people think it fictitious I shall refrain.

Johnson had strong views about 'minding his belly', and would have eagerly enquired about the kind of food that he could expect. I am neutral in this context and confess to liking all Mediterranean food from squids to aubergines, from cévapčići to avgolemono. The wine of the Mediterranean has improved out of all recognition in the last fifty years. Sicilian wine used to be a laughing-stock, apart from Marsala; now both there and in Cyprus you will find a most drinkable standard steadily maintained or, rather, annually advanced.

In the old days, guidebooks used to be as dictatorial as the Great Cham himself, telling you exactly what you should feel in response to the various sights with which you are faced. The modern style is more permissive. It would have suited a young American I knew, who confessed privately that she could never remember whether the Acropolis was on top of the Parthenon or the Parthenon on top of the Acropolis; or the Englishman whose response to Arthur Evans's *art-nouveau* reconstruction of the Palace of Knossos was, 'Call this Crete, I call it concrete.' Does this mean the modern tourist is more of a philistine? I doubt it: the Reverend Francis Kilvert, the Victorian diarist, deserted his clerical character so far as to write: 'Of all noxious animals the most noxious is a tourist; and of all tourists the most vulgar, ill-bred, offensive and loathsome is the British tourist. No wonder dogs fly at them.' This was, be it noted, before the popularity of football.

It cannot be concealed, and the philologist Johnson would have relished it, that a number of languages are spoken on the shores of the Mediterranean, many of which present difficulties to the English-speaker. Of all the problems facing the traveller this may be rated the least. It is not true that the British are specially bad at foreign languages; the average Frenchman is far more stubbornly monoglot. There still remain, though, plenty of traces of the once dominant position of French, which was the second official language of the Ottoman Empire. There is a tendency to treat English as though it could be easily vamped by anyone who knows French. In a church in Amarante in northern Portugal last October I came across a tri-lingual notice in which the Portuguese and French texts were impeccable but the English read 'Every one is prayed to slip only in the boxes their offering.' But my favourite memory is of a notice in the Museum at Olympia fifty years ago. The Greek and French were all right; English-speakers were warned: 'The honourable the voyagers are defended to crash, to fume or to photograph out the objects.'

September 1985

'Mr Oliphant is on holiday. He'll be back looking disgustingly tanned and healthy and nauseatingly full of beans, on August 27th.'

7

MY CUP OF TEA

THE BRITISH CHARACTER
Importance of Tea

'I assure you we use only French additives.'

'I've forgotten again! Do we have red or white wine with the fish?'

Humphrey Lyttelton

THE PICNIC PAPERS

The one really essential rule about a picnic is that you should ward off, with the ferocity of a tigress defending her young, the advice of any twit who thinks he can tell you how to make the most of a picnic. Having a picnic is one of those activities, like keeping a diary, which you must do in your own way or not at all. The *Concise Oxford Dictionary* is delightfully vague about the word 'picnic' itself. It mumbles something about a 'pleasure party including meal out of doors,' gives the derivation as *pique-nique* (which is just saying the same thing in a Maurice Chevalier accent) and then hurries on to 'picot,' 'picotee,' 'picquet' and 'picric' with never a backward glance.

'Pleasure party including meal out of doors' seems to me to cover an almost limitless range of *al fresco* fun. But typically, the British make rather a fuss – a pique-nique mystique, if you like – about eating out of doors. The Catering Manager of BEA once told me that the whole of flight catering today is based on the observable fact that, regardless of when or how much he last ate, a passenger's first thought once the aircraft's wheels leave the runway is 'Where's the food?'

It's much the same with the British and the open air – one whiff of bracken or glimpse of rabbit-droppings and it's out with the hamper and let's get stuck in. We have even managed, in our own inimitable way, to imbue the whole affair with several sorts of snobbery. We have *haute pique-nique* experts in the glossy mags to tell us how to make interesting sandwiches out of caviar and salmon leftovers and which Sauterne will go best with the peaches without attracting too many wasps. I suspect that few people pay attention to them. For our attitude to the picnic is Stoic rather than Epicurean.

The real picnic snob is the man who uses the event to show his contempt for civilisation in all its forms. He looks back to some mythical Golden Age when all men were boy scouts in flappy khaki shorts, fending for themselves without the aid of any of your namby-pamby modern inventions. ('That's you!' cried my family in unison when I read them this paragraph, but I don't see it. For one thing, my shorts are not flapping khaki but rather natty David Niven jobs – or were before somebody confiscated them.) According to the picnic snob's code, Bracken and Twigs take precedence over Newspaper and Kindling Wood, Newspaper and Kindling Wood over Primus, Primus over Camping Gas, Camping Gas over Portable Barbecue and everything over Collapsible Table and Tea Cosy.

I have to tell him that history, insofar as we can interpret it from Art and Literature, is not on his side. I suppose Manet's famous *Déjeuner sur l'Herbe* was a picnic within the meaning of the act, and whatever those glum-looking men in Sunday attire are up to with that naked lady in their midst, it certainly isn't roughing it.

In practically every classic English novel I ever read there is a point where one of the characters, presumably fed up with loafing about through two hundred and sixty pages without actually doing a thing, suggests a picnic and the lady of the house claps her hands and cries 'Yes, a picnic it shall be!' Next morning, with a lot of female twittering and male flirting, a fleet of carriages sets off for some distant spot on the estate where the servants, presumably working all night, have erected tables, spread linen and set out a sumptuous repast. It must be noted that our heroes and heroines do not spend the morning scrabbling about for twigs, puffing like human bellows into a heap of lukewarm ashes, covering their finery with spitting fat and indulging in recriminations about who did or did not pack the salt. Their day, and the author's chapter, is spent eating a few refined mouthfuls, playing ball, wandering off into the shrubbery and generally, if rather tortuously, getting on with the plot.

If this is the genuine, prototype picnic – and it seems to fit the COD's definition pretty well – then we must accept that the leisurely repast in a layby off the A5, with the collapsible table erected in the lee of the Ford Anglia, fish paste in lieu of duck pâté and a tin-opener in lieu of servants, with Dad snoozing, Mum knitting, Gran watching the cars go by and the kids picking blackberries or trying to get Rover to do his business before the next leg of the journey, comes much closer to it than your boy scout safari. But as I said at the outset, a picnic is what you make of it, and if you want to make it an adventure-substitute, a military exercise involving the defusing of exploding sausages

and the dodging of flying fat shrapnel, then good luck and don't fire till you see the whites of their eggs.

Me, I've done it all. When I was a schoolboy, my mother used to take me and a few chums on fry-ups in Windsor Great Park, cooking bacon in great lumps of lard and spicing the fried eggs with charred bracken. It all tasted lovely. The nearest I ever came to *haute pique-nique*, I suppose, was when as a young officer in the Grenadier Guards at Windsor I was sent, with five colleagues, to camp for three days by the Thames at Marlow, presumably as some sort of toughening-up exercise. The Officers' Mess Sergeant at Victoria Barracks sent with us three huge packing cases full of food, drink, cutlery and crockery – and in the true picnic tradition, he forgot to pack anything to go with the gin. So we drank six bottles of port on the first night, researching the theory that (*a*) you get drunk quicker and (*b*) you have less of a hangover in the open air. Nobody thought to put a stopwatch on the proceedings, so when one of our number got up to go to his tent and walked, with a silly smile

'No, please, it's quite all right.
Saves me plucking them.'

on his face, fully-dressed into the Thames, we were unable – incapable is perhaps the word – to come up with any conclusive findings. As for the hangover, we all agreed in the early morning that we felt remarkably fit. There were even occasional cries of 'Yippee!' which suggested that the hangover, so far from departing silently, had not yet arrived.

Picnicking is, alas, not what it used to be. It's all very well to curl the lip as you roar on your way to some comfy roadhouse past the typical British family eating and enjoying the fresh fumes by the roadside. It could well be me and my lot, fully equipped with everything from matches and kindling wood to gas cooker and portable wine cooler, warding off starvation after five hours' fruitless search in, say, Dorset or Cambridgeshire or the New Forest or even Windsor Great Park of blessed memory for just a few square feet of open, non-barbed-wired, non-hedged, non-gated-and-padlocked country in which to commune with nature and fry a banger. It was all right for Jane Austen and the Brontës and the rest of them – with a stroke of the pen they could have their

characters owning half the countryside. As far as I'm concerned they still do.

I take it out once a year on the mountains of Wales (Scotland or the remoter Lake District would do as well) where, a few hundred feet above sea level, the loose stone walls peter out and you can roam at will with no one but sheep to watch your absurd goings-on. As for the future, it lies perhaps in communal picnicking in the old tradition. Already we have the Picnic Areas designated for it. The Germans, one stage ahead and bowing presumably to what they deem to be the inevitable, have for some years been furnishing their laybys with wooden tables and benches, all ready for communal sausage-slicing, *Stein*-tipping and martial song-singing.

Personally, if there is one square inch of this green and pleasant land still showing through the tarmac, I shall be there, charring it black.

March 1972

"All right, who'd like a jacket potato?"

HIS BITTER HALF

John. 'DRINK 'EARTY, MARIA. DRINK WIRRY NIGH 'ARF.'

'No, Lawrence – four shish and two doner, one with onions and one without. No saveloys.'

Fay Maschler

KNIVES AT THE ROUND TABLE

One of the visions I had before marriage was of me giving dinner parties. Of course, I had had people to dinner before, but being a part of a married couple invested the process with a different aura. In the fantasy I wore, for some reason, a vaguely oriental dress. I smiled a lot and glided about. Sometimes I stood at the head of the table and looked down on everyone having a marvellous time and gave a particular sort of benign smile. I didn't seem to know anyone very well but the guests were good-looking and interesting, and it almost goes without saying, successful. Although I was only what strikes me now as a tiresome glowing presence, the whole event somehow emanated from me; the conversations were silken threads that I rippled and wove and knotted and occasionally snipped. Of course it has never been like that.

Dinner parties are one of the penalties of marriage, or indeed of being a couple; rather than having your very own friends over for a meal, the deal becomes one of diplomacy and trading and pay-offs. You soon discover that one or other of you takes exception to most of your old friends and even when you have decided on a guest-list there begins what still strikes me as the insuperable problem of getting everyone together on the same evening.

Unless you plan the thing months ahead, which has all kinds of disadvantages like forgetting you invited them, and instilling in the guests the feeling that it is going to be a grand and important affair (I was very taken aback once when a woman obviously used to a superior class of do rang beforehand to ask what I would be wearing), and then forgetting they are supposed to come, meanwhile having found something more enticing to do – you are left with the scenario of ringing up A who can come and then B who can come and then C who can't and so you have to ring A again and suggest another date which A can do but B can't. There is no solution but compromise.

The mix of people is, of course, paramount. Logic and good sense would indicate that having hit on a congenial group you would ask them back again and again and having devised a popular menu you would cook it time after time. But dinner parties are not for such obvious unalloyed pleasures. Oh, no.

As H. L. Mencken put it, 'The capacity of human beings to bore one another seems to be vastly greater than that of any other animal. Some of their most esteemed inventions have no other apparent purpose, for example the dinner party of more than two, the epic poem and the science of metaphysics.' A mistake is to invite too many people who consider themselves witty and entertaining or are. They are immediately deeply bored by the presence of each other, for what good is a joke if it just falls on another joke? Some years ago we had Mr and Mrs Kurt Vonnegut, Mr and Mrs Kenneth Tynan, Mr and Mrs Trevor Nunn and Martin Amis to dinner. For a good deal of the time they stared glumly at their plates.

On the whole, people want to see their friends but dinner parties are designed to put a stop to that; you are there to make new contacts and acquaintances. A theory put forward at a dinner party I went to recently is that you are more likely to do so at a rectangular table than a circular one. With the aid of diagrams the proponent of this notion demonstrated that at a circular table you can, at most, speak to two people, unless you want to bellow loudly or lean back precariously in your chair. Many more lines, criss-crosses and arrows symbolised chat at the rectangular table. So there is the first consideration before entertaining.

Food and drink is another item worth some study. Although *Tatler* editor Mark Boxer said, when approached on the subject of food, that it was his feeling that no one ate any more, I have found that when people come to dinner they expect a little something. This is borne out by the fact that there has arisen a branch of cooking referred to as dinner party food.

Just as you are not supposed to invite people you really like, it is not deemed correct to offer the food you normally enjoy. Steak is an example of something you might like. Beef Wellington, where the steak is smeared with pâté or a mixture of chopped mushrooms or both and wrapped in pastry, thereby creating a cookery snare since the meat and the pastry require different cooking times, is an example of Dinner Party Food.

Countless magazine articles are written to advise the cook about preparing for the dinner party. This generally entails starting three days ahead and a lot of Clingfilm. It avoids what in my life I call the chapatti factor – which refers to me standing in the kitchen 45 minutes after everyone has arrived, enveloped in a cloud of grimy smoke cooking little discs of unleavened bread in a dry, iron frying-pan because it has occurred to me that they will go well with the first course.

It can lead, however, to systems like one I encountered where the hostess had employed first the Kenwood to make soups, various savoury purées coloured pink and green, and similarly recondite sweetened messes for dessert, and frozen them, masses of them, to be thawed as needed for dinner parties. It was said about her that she had a file index of these dishes all numbered. She herself confided to me towards the end of one meal that using margarine, green beans

and sugar in the liquidiser she had made a very good green bean ice-cream.

In my view, unless you know that the people you are entertaining care a lot about food – in itself fairly paralysing – it is foolish to go to a great deal of trouble because they will not notice, will mistake what you have cooked for something else, will reach for their cigarettes before the first course has made it back from the dining table to the kitchen sink, will fall asleep because they have had a very tiring day, will announce they are on a diet that allows only salt-free cooking or will be too drunk to manœuvre the food from the plate to their mouth.

The last can happen when the cooking is ambitious for you will have miscalculated the time it takes to stuff okra with a spicy onion mixture and still be at it – coaxing a teaspoonful between the slit in the tiny little pods – when people arrive. Also, though I am guilty of doing it nearly every time, if you cook elaborately and intensively the guests become a terrible anti-climax.

If you have not made too much effort it is easier to cope with any reactions to the food including rudeness. A friend of mine who is an accomplished cook told me of an occasion when the wife of someone she had asked announced upon arrival that she had a headache and asked for two aspirins. These Jane

smilby.

gave her in the form of the pills that dissolve in water, saying, 'I'm afraid these don't taste very nice.' 'They'll taste a lot better than anything else one eats in this house,' replied the woman. It is at these moments that the concept of graciousness is tested in any hostess.

Perhaps for some reasons like the above, or equally for reasons of finance, the dinner party as an activity seems to be on the decline. There seems to be a breakdown in that sort of compulsory hospitality where there has to be a return match, a response to what was served to you, as if in a tedious game of social tennis.

Women who once thought it proper to spend the day barding shoulders of veal with strips of pork back fat that had been rolled in finely chopped fresh herbs and hand-ground black pepper now probably spend the after-noon at the cinema or run an advertising agency. Having caterers – proof that both the man and woman are in vital professions – has not caught on here as it has in New York and Los Angeles, perhaps because no one can face the smoked mackerel mousse, *coq au vin* and chilled lemon soufflé that the Sloanes who graduate from cookery schools will provide.

Anyway, if you add the expense of help to the expense of the food and the prodigious quantities of drink that always get consumed, a dinner party becomes an investment, a shaky one, even in terms of being asked back.

I read somewhere that in the South-West of England there was a fashion for dinner parties where each guest brought a course; either that or you hurtled from house to house, I can't remember. What I find does work well is if you have a friend you like who makes good desserts and she brings one.

That way, if you have done all the shop-ping and cooking, there will be one course you won't be numbingly familiar with. Whatever she makes probably won't unbal-ance your meal. It cuts down on some of the

'Pshaw, it's evaporated!'

planning and work and gives you a chance to feel like a guest for a while, rather than the harassed, hostile hostess the sweet Eastern beauty of my imaginings has become.

April 1984

Michael Bywater

BADLY SHAKEN

When the wasp stings and the teeth break, then is the season to sing 'Hey Nonny Not

As Such, But I Do Remember Your Brother' but whatever you do *don't breathe in*, chances being that you are head down in a reeking firkin 'of vicious cogenerics which taken directly into the lungs could lead to a more permanent version of that oblivion which we all crave.

(Hello hello, how nice, yes isn't it lovely, I say that looks good I certainly will ... Is it? How clever. And crème-de-menthe as well? Really! Well it's certainly refreshing ... yes, I bet it packs a punch ha ha ha oh gosh there's Titus, haven't seen him for years ... Did he? Who to? No, I wasn't invited, actually we've lost touch, I gather he's doing very well in, um, accountancy, I'll just pop over and ...)

A clever trick, the cocktail. The crazed one-man-band of dissonant tastes is carefully designed, not for pleasure on the palate (for there is no cocktail, even the Dry Martini, which can be regarded as anything other than depraved) but to stun the taste-buds into submission and thus fool the brain into the sort of misconception that loses wars. 'Nothing so nasty,' says the brain, 'could be also poisonous, so there is no need to worry.'

And the defences are down, and vigilance sleeps, and the enemy rushes in, and the next thing you know you are lying in a strange bath wearing a crash helmet, smoking a rosary and wondering what happened and who with.

THE BRITISH CHARACTER
ABSOLUTE INDISPENSABILITY OF BACON AND EGGS FOR BREAKFAST

The last bit is important. The hidden purpose of the cocktail is to promote illicit lubricity which, again, it does by stealth. Eros and the burning fiery pit are ill-served by, say, sherry. One does not hear of wild illegal couplings occurring after a glass or two of decent hock. And not surprisingly. The business is such a mug's game that it's better to drink a good bottle or two. But after a couple of Horse's Necks or whatever, even so tacky an alternative as sneaking under the duvet with someone else's ghastly wife seems better than having another bloody Horse's Neck.

(*Titus! How's accountancy? It is accountancy, isn't it? Oh. Is there a lot of call for containers? It sounds fascinating. And this must be your ... Jessica! What a charming name. How long have you ... Three months, eh! Well done. Yes, get me one too while you're there, old chap. Tell me, Jessica ...*)

Must, of course, be someone else's wife. There's something fundamentally seedy about filling up on Wall Street Crashes and then lurching unsteadily towards your own wife, leering greenishly and groping about like one of those melancholy creatures that live in the sea. Come to think about it, there's also something not quite on about drinking cocktails at home. It goes against the ethos.

It's quite clear why, of course. The cocktail was the tipple of choice of the Bright Young Things, for whom being alone was anathema, and the resonances have stuck. A quiet uxorious Sidecar is as unthinkable as wearing a mitre to an orgy, partly because a cocktail is generally so disagreeable that you only drink it to show off, but mainly because of the subtextual meanings hidden in that bitter and aromatic cup.

Structuralists, who are now unfashionable and therefore OK, might reveal to suckers like you and me that a cocktail is a sort of bibulous encapsulation of role-confusion in a mobile society. Humble gin is yoked to outlandish liquor and intolerant bitters, and

the resulting glass, while poisoning (and secretly disgusting) the consumer, nevertheless signals that he can conjoin the various incompatible elements and produce a satisfactory status display. Structuralists say the same thing about a lot of things, like children's stories, and you can see their point: compared with some of the lethalities served up at the Algonquin bar, a few pages of *Winnie-the-Pooh* ripped out and scrunched up in a glass would be almost agreeable, and much better for you.

(*Here you are, hee hee hee, whoops, gosh this stuff packs quite a kick ... Well, Jessica, you make me very sad. Why? Because I wish I'd met you before. A long time before. Don't look at me like that. You have quite wonderful eyes. Between you and me, Titus is a bit of a bore, but of course you won't think that. Yet. You do? Doesn't he? Good God. If I were in his shoes, I'd ...*)

Perhaps that's why the cocktail has become the drink of the upwardly mobile young, who hang around places like Zanzibar and all points downward drinking the bloody things and talking about their BMWs, the sort of people who are carefully classless and dress like someone else and buy Georgian terraced houses and install black Venetian blinds and fill their rooms with ghastly 'witty' artefacts bought at Camden Lock – the very things, probably, that their parents got rid of back in 1954. There's a sort of sneering, eager feeling about them, and they shout and laugh and listen to Buddy Holly and are 'in' design or graphics or photography or television and are pretty horrid, really.

(*Don't cry, Jessica, please ... you need some fresh air, come for a stroll round the garden, Tight-arse will never notish ... oh did I? Just an old nickname to show our contempt, hur hur ... yes, it is, isn't it. He is, isn't he? Here ... let's pop through this door ...*)

And the paraphernalia appeals, too, to some childish instinct innate in cocktail drinkers. The coloured straws. The rows of little bottles. The daft bloody glasses with a tube coming out of the bottom and coiling round changing colour, so that it's like drinking hemlock out of some B-movie mad scientist's atom-smasher. The things with batteries in that wizz up your drinks. The witty pastiche ice-buckets. All that flannel and visual rodomontade. I suppose it makes up for the fact that they have no palate; do they turn, later in life, into those sorts of awful bores who buy wine gadgets like cellar humidifiers and brass-and-mahogany decanting machines with crank and candle ('Our ewn tasterres always use zis machine, so now we 'ave decided to make eet avellable to the publique...') but can't tell a Sancerre from a Mersault? I suppose they must. Nothing worse, really, unless it's rolling a cigar between finger and thumb *without any idea whatsoever why you're doing it.*

(*'Salright, 'sjust aroun, sroun, sroun, sroun, 'sjusroun the corner, I'zhe give you cup of coff nthen w'll pop back, you'll fell mush better darling. Here, hole donter my arm, my arm, hnuh, erp...*)

No, sorry. It's not really on. The cocktail stultifies the brain, constricts the speech, eats like acid into the morals, furs the tongue, causes the eye to bleed, consumes with

Nurse. 'Miss Joan and Master John have been so naughty, Madam, I'm sure I don't know what to do with them.'
Mother. 'Of course you must punish them. Send 'em to bed without their cocktails.'

*'I don't usually drink this amount,
but I've got my foot trapped.'*

Angus Wilson

PARTIES: BEING A HOST

reproach, dulls the wits and hurts the head. The only one which has anything resembling a reputation is the Dry Martini. Do you want to know how to make one? This is funny, this, it's a good one, this is, I think you'll like this. Take three measures of gin and pour over crushed ice. Take the top off a bottle of vermouth and, holding the gin, walk past the vermouth bottle...

When? You've heard it? No you haven't. When you have walked past the vermouth bottle, *keep on walking*. Walk into your kitchen, throw the gin down the sink, open a bottle of cool hock, and drink something decent for a change. That is the secret of a perfect Martini.

(*O Dzheshicca Dzheshicca your shin isw like skilk you are the mosffffffffff Dhis iv ahslutely wonful. Hazt bin like thi for you too? Withzzzzzzzzzzzzzzzzzzzzzzz. I love you too but whvvvvvvvvvv AK! Nnnnner! O God o God o God not again itz the ori ori olives they never agreed with ORRRRP! HOOF! o God...*)

June 1984

You can give two kinds of cocktail parties – those that 'go too far' or those that 'never really get started.' You can tell which kind you gave the next day when your best friends ring up to thank you. 'I'm afraid last night's party...' you say hesitantly down the telephone. There is just that perceptible pause which tells you that your friend Cora Campbellfoot is summoning all her 'good scout' loyalty together and wants you to know it.

Then, twice as bright as life, she screams down the 'phone: 'Nonsense, darling. It was a *wild* success. I got the impression everyone was enjoying themselves *madly*.' Once again there is a slight pause and then, 'I don't think you could *possibly* have stopped Sybil Applerot from having so much, if that's what's worrying you. But it *is* a pity, of course, because she does such *silly* things...' *Like slopping a whole gin over my new coat and skirt.* 'Harry said to thank you very much. He enjoyed himself enormously. And the youngest Tomtom boy came round with his overcoat this morning, so *that* was all right.' *He got soaked to the skin finding a taxi, but...* 'It was sweet of you, darling, to let us bring Ann. Her first grown-up party. We wondered if that Nicaraguan *quite* realized she was only just sixteen, but...' *As it is, the morning post has already brought a most unsuitable invitation to the seaside, and she's given him her school address, so heaven knows!* ... Your party, in fact, went too far.

On the other hand, if it never really got going, Cora's reassuring coo down the receiver will tell you so straight away. 'Of course not, dear. Harry and I thought it was a *lovely* little party. It was so nice to see such a lot of old friends again. I had *such* a long chat with Maimie Mappin ...' *One hour, to be exact, and she was no whit altered since we christened her little Miss Dreary for* 1931. 'Oh my dear! don't worry about *that*. You can trust Harry to look after himself.' *He certainly had to; he says he had one refill in an hour and a half, and that was with iced nail varnish.* 'Ann? Oh, no, dear, not unhappy. She always cries when she's over-excited. I'm afraid she's a bit young yet for grownup parties.' *All the same, to be left for over an hour with Colonel Plimmer would be something of an ordeal for Elsa Maxwell herself. I should have cried with sheer boredom hours before ...* Your party was really a non-starter.

Once, however, you have decided whether you want your party to go too far or to hang fire it's fairly easy to make sure of either effect. For a really slow party, there's nothing like 'cup' – either the cold, sticky variety with a vegetable flotsam or the lukewarm sort usually known as 'punch.' If you do decide on 'cup,' however, remember that it's catching, and that if you live in any but a very wide social circle there's liable to be a 'lot of cup about' at parties you go to for some time to come. 'We were so fascinated by the claret cup you gave us last week that we've tried one of our own. Only we've added Demerara sugar and willow herb. We *hope* you'll think it's an improvement.'

You can't really expect them not to want to get their own back. But to obtain the full flattening effect of 'cup' there is nothing like a New Year's Eve party. A basis of heavy, cheap red wine and cold tea will guarantee that even those business acquaintances from Hendon, whose jokes tend to be as 'near the knuckle' as they are pointless, or 'fast' little Mrs Piggott, whose high spirits have gathered speed ever since her divorce way back in 1925, will be yawning their heads off in half an hour. And they *all have to stay there until midnight.* That's the glory of it. Even the dark man who goes out to greet the New Year with greenery may well fall asleep on the snow-covered doorstep. For a really dead party there's nothing like New Year's Eve on 'cup.'

To get a party to 'go too far,' of course, requires more expenditure. But with the right guests you can still do quite a lot on comparatively little drink. A good basis can be found in the Brashers, that childless couple we all know, eternally young, eternally back-chatting, becoming 'uncle' and 'aunt' to more and more of their friends' children as the years pass them by. The Brashers have always been out for fun rather than responsibility, and fun they'll see they have on the noisiest possible terms. Watch her shout 'Ugly Mug' across to her husband, and he replying with 'Tuppence' or 'Buttons' or 'Where's that ghastly woman of mine?' For ever Myrna Loy and William Powell in the *Thin Man* era. Their jolly, legpulling flirtation can usually be relied on to end in a good stand-up scene before the party's over. With a little cheap champagne, the Brashers and a blonde for him to get off with, your party will have gone too far before it's time for dinner.

April 1953

8
MAN'S BEST FRIENDS

Lady Visitor. 'I SEE YOU STILL HAVE POOR OLD BINGO.'
Fair Widow. 'YES. I WOULDN'T PART WITH HIM ON ANY ACCOUNT. I NEVER LOOK AT HIM WITHOUT THINKING OF POOR DEAR MARMADUKE!'

George Melly

CUB REPORTER

The holidays have started after a most hectic and diverse early July. I'm at the Tower, nerve-ends unravelling, taking in great gulps of sleep, the adrenalin level going down like the mercury in a thermometer after a fever. Even the weather, a gale this morning, thin rain this afternoon, seems like a benison.

Nevertheless, the Tower is haunted this late summer by a small, lithe spectre: sharp-nosed, amber-eyed, needle-toothed. Its name is James. In April Beryl Fury, the formidable miner's wife whom we met last summer during the strike, offered Diana a fox-cub to look after. Its mother had been killed and Ms Fury, whose love of animals is equal to her dislike of Mrs T., was unable to take it on. Besides innumerable other creatures, she has a fox of her own who, although adult and wild, still pays her the odd sociable visit and wouldn't take kindly to a new pretender to her affections. So James arrived; a round, sweet-smelling bundle, bluish-brown and more kitten-like than foxy.

When I first heard I was initially resistant. It seemed somehow very 'Sixtyish' to have a fox, but once I'd seen it I was as besotted as everyone else. He was named 'James Fox', not after the actor, but in homage to the author of *White Mischief* who has often stayed with us. This has sometimes led to a certain linguistic confusion.

I didn't see as much of James as Diana and the children – an abnormally busy schedule curtailed my occasional visits to Wales – but he made several trips to London so I was very much aware of the rapid emergence of the wild creature from the helpless bundle; the black-tipped ears bigger, the muzzle

'A few years ago you never saw a fox in the suburbs.'

longer, the tail, tipped with white, less stumpy. His movements, too; sudden leaps sideways, rapid withdrawal when startled, instant silent materialisations, a loping trot around and over the furniture evoked the wild-wood rather than the living-room. There was no way then that James could be confused with puppy or kitten, although in some respects he seemed poised between cat and dog. Strangely enough, though, from his earliest waddling days he was self-house-trained, almost meticulous in his use of the litter tray. Early on, he developed a suspicion of strange men but an instant trust of women. It took him some time to tolerate me, but he eventually proved his acceptance, when in London, by springing out from a cupboard in the basement, where he had established his 'earth' in a hole under the sink, and nipping me playfully on the ankle as I tottered to the bathroom for an early morning pee. Here, too, if I wasn't very sharp in closing the door, and he moved like lightning, he would take a rather embarrassing

interest in this function, resting his front paws on the rim of the basin until I had finished.

His passion, here at least puppy-like, was for footwear. My pair of disreputable but much-cherished slippers vanished into the hole under the sink, although oddly enough *one* of them was later returned more or less intact. This was his pattern, to destroy one; a detective examining our shoes would have reached the bizarre conclusion that we were a household of one-legged persons. He could be naughty but, as Diana pointed out, while making himself judiciously scarce after the event, he showed absolutely no guilt. Domestic pets are stained by our awareness of sin. Not so James. He predated the fall of man.

As he grew bigger a dreadful decision began to loom. It is possible to castrate a fox, thereby avoiding not only its powerful scent but also its primitive urges, and to bring it up as a pet. This was never in question, but to drive him off from the Tower would have been a death-sentence. Initially he would

'It's the cat – he'll be late. Can we leave something out.'

have been too trusting, his reward to be shot or trapped, and besides there is a local hunt.

Diana's first attempt to find him a halfway house was a failure; a well-meaning, hippy-ish, animal-rights commune in Essex called 'Bright and Beautiful', whose notion of weaning James to the wild was to shut him in a dirty shed for a few weeks and then abruptly set him free. She left him overnight with grave misgivings and returned next day to hear him howling for her. She reclaimed him, but only after he had fled to the woods for several panic-stricken hours. It took him ages to regain his confidence and, on the way back to the Tower, he bit her companion, an unheard-of transgression until that moment.

Finally, she discovered some foresters with a practical love and knowledge of wild creatures and, sadly but gratefully, entrusted James into their hands. He has graduated there from a kennel-run, via a deer-enclosure, to the woods, taking her slipper with him. He returns, secretly, to remove food they leave out for him. It must be him; no totally wild fox would enter a wired in, trap-like space. There is no hunt nearby, no farmers. He has every chance of survival in those virgin woods.

He will gradually forget us all, even Diana, but we, and especially Diana, will never forget him. He is certainly the best documented fox in history. There are dozens of photographs of him at every stage: leaping, worrying objects, sleeping, strutting across the back of a sofa. My step-daughter Candy has celebrated him in a little book called *Red Mischief* in which these images are reinforced by suitable quotes from poets and writers. Meanwhile, we hope and believe James to be emulating Ted Hughes's *Thought Fox*:

> *Across clearings, an eye,*
> *A widening deepening greenness,*
> *Brilliantly, concentratedly,*
> *Coming about its own business.*

August 1985

'*Now the three-point turn . . .*'

'Stupid idiot! That mare could have broken a leg.'

Thelwell

A GOD CALLED HORSE

'You little beast – you've been eating Tonto's peppermint creams.'

'Catch the rope, Alice, catch the rope and tie it firmly round his neck.'

'Keep calm, woman – you're making him nervous.'

'I don't think I'd mind so much if it was another woman.'

*'**Alison!** I think he wants a drink of water.'*

Alex Atkinson

KUDDLE KORNER

Auntie Amy, who knows all the Funny Ways of Little Doggies, answers your Anxious Queries

Q. There seems to be something the matter with Mrs Miniver, my dachshund. She is eighteen and a half. Her eyesight is failing, and sometimes she isn't sure who I am. Also she cannot walk any more, because her tum-tum brushes along the ground and she weighs ever such a lot. Another thing is her breathing: she snuffles a great deal at the foot of my bed, where she lives, and this keeps me awake. Sometimes I think she is unhappy. My vet has no sympathy for me. I won't *tell* you what he suggests. Can you help me?

ELEANOR P., W.1

A. What Mrs Miniver needs is a change of atmosphere. Since she cannot walk, why

'Who's a pretty boy, then?'

not get her a little cart? I saw a sweet one only the other day, in old rose and eau-de-nil, with a tiny folding hood in case the naughty rain-drops decide to pitter-pat! There were tartan reins for Mummy to pull, and a dear little blanket with matching pillow. I'm sure she would enjoy her 'walkies' in such an elegant carriage, and it would give her a new outlook on life. Remember that if we really *try*, we can make our doggies last *ever* such a long time. As for her eyesight, have you thought of glasses at all?

Q. My baby goldfish keeps his mouth open all the time, and I fear he may fill with water and pass away. Is there something I can do?

Mrs R., Crouch End

JULIUS II
1962-1974

A. I know nothing of goldfish. I sometimes feel it is cruel to keep them. Perhaps he has lockjaw.

Q. How selfish people are! Yesterday I got on a bus with my dear little poodle, and had to go upstairs. Jo-Jo *loves* to look out of the window, but do you think the horrid woman by whom we had to sit would change places? She refused point-blank. She had an appalling little boy on her lap, who wasn't even *interested in looking* out of the window: he just kept munching his awful sticky sweets and pulling faces at poor Jo-Jo. Such a dreadful little boy, too, with ragged clothes, and marks all over his legs where someone had hit him with a stick, and hardly any flesh on his bones. Why he wasn't at school I can't think, but since he couldn't articulate properly I suppose that didn't matter. I did feel proud of my Jo-Jo, sitting on my lap as good as gold, with his nice new ribbon and his *Toujours l'Amour* perfume. The people on the bus noticed the difference too, for there was many a pat on the head for Jo-Jo as they passed, and many a frown for the awful little boy. I was *ever* so glad when Jo-Jo eventually knocked all the sweets on to the floor (he's very intelligent) and then jumped down and *sat* on them! How the people round about did smile! The awful woman could do nothing but snivel. Wasn't it clever of Jo-Jo to pay her out for her selfishness!

Mrs M., Hampstead

A. Yes, very. And thank you for the snap. He certainly is a credit to you.

Q. I am worried about my peke, Candy. Sometimes in the evening she will not talk to me, and spits at Mary Malcolm. I feel we are slowly drifting apart, and yet I know she does not really hate me. It's just that life is losing its zest for her.

Lily F., Bath

A. Why not try a tasty supper-snack? Something different – exciting! For instance: A pound of fillet steak stewed in any good Graves. Cut into teeny slices, and serve with a sauce made from the rest of the wine, chopped braised mushrooms (*not* the stalks), minced asparagus tips, and a few truffles. Always remember that our doggies feel the strain of these difficult days just as much as we do, and a gay surprise now and then works wonders.

'Take your leg out of my dog's mouth, you monster!'

Q. The woman next door has no doggie, but two years ago she gave birth to a human child. Recently she has taken to walking down the street whenever I am in the garden, with the child in her arms as though it were a doggie. One day she had tied a big bow round its neck, and yesterday I'll swear it was wearing a *collar*. My Rufus barks at them whenever he sees them, but it has no effect. I know that soon she will walk past with the child on a *leash*, and I shall go out of my *mind*. What can I do?

PHYLLIS D., High Barnet

A. Ignore her. She is jealous. Alternatively, move to Kensington.

Q. Often when I am standing at bus stops strange women kiss my Audrey. I do not like to discourage this, because Audrey is naturally affectionate, and I should hate her to become repressed. But I sometimes wonder if it is really good for her?

R.P. (MISS), Kew

A. Definitely not. If too many people kiss your doggie, she may become confused in her little mind as to who actually loves her. This could lead either to an anxiety neurosis or to promiscuity. Besides, you never know where some people have *been*.

Q. I read in the paper about a confounded poodle called Grandma attending a cocktail party, shaking hands all round, drinking dry Martinis, and having its toenails painted light green to match its mistress's. What the devil are we coming to?

LT-COL. F., Bournemouth

A. What indeed? Light green is not a shade *I* would recommend for a poodle – and Grandma is rather a frivolous name, I feel.

Q. I am at my wits' end about my cocker spaniel, Rover. He simply will *not* be carried when we go for walkies, and he seems to resent it when I put on his sweet little duffel coat on windy days. He runs about in a very

'I notice he's my tortoise when he misbehaves.'

rough way if I am not careful, and has recently taken to *barking*. On more than one occasion he has chased little pussy-cats, and he *refuses* to sit quietly on his chair in a restaurant. He is getting quite a big puppy now.

NANCY T., W.C.1

A. You really must persevere, dear. It is our duty to teach our doggies the proper way to behave. Try keeping him locked indoors for a few weeks – in one room if possible. Once you have broken his unruly spirit it should not be difficult to make a nice, quiet, lovable doggie out of him. Keep him on a diet of potted shrimps and chocolate creams. And don't despair. Always remember that you hold a trump card: your doggie trusts and respects you, and *knows* that everything you do is for his own good.

February 1955

Richard Gordon

A BEDSIDE DOG

All my family being medical, none enjoys the faintest sympathy when falling ill. It is probably the same among the Rothschilds when one goes broke, and among a family of professional thieves when one gets nicked.

I woke with a splitting headache, a high temperature and peculiar rose-red spots. My kin crowded round the bed, poked and groped and swapped opinions, like the students in the wards at Barts.

We had a terrible family argument whether it was typhoid, or flu with bites from the dog's fleas. Then they disappeared to lavish sympathy on strangers, as they were paid to.

A scratching at the bedroom door. The dog himself, my orange belton English setter, Thackeray. We artists value our dogs by naming them after our greats (my neighbour the musician calls his poodle Offenbach). They are the only creatures an Englishman can be blatantly sentimental over, unlike over his wife.

Thackeray sat at my bedside, compassion thick as treacle in his brown eyes, concern dripping like the spittle from his chops.

This is the latest therapy from the Royal College of Nursing.

The lady from the PRO Dogs National Charity showed the nurses her own English setter, Poppy, also her 12-stone Irish wolfhound, who does not sound so cosy. She says that extrovert dogs who like meeting strangers make wonderful health visitors.

Furry Florence Nightingales act better than a visit from the doctor, many people finding it easier to communicate with dumb animals than with doctors.

PRO Dogs has 800 straining at the leash, which would serve a large hospital and create a pleasant change from the bleak boredom of ward life as they growled worrying the sterile towels, barked at the consultants in the doorway, lifted their legs against the beds and bit the hands which fed the patients.

I gently pulled my nurse's ears. He has so reassuring a bedside manner. I spend longer in Thackeray's company than my family's. He is at my feet, or wherever I want to put them, as I am writing, dozing away the evening or going walkies in the woods. When in Wordsworthian reverie I one day trip on a root and break my neck, I hope he will

'Leave me if you must, Marjorie, but to run away with my best friend, that's what really hurts.'

howl heartbreakingly over my corpse until the National Trust arrive to clear away the litter.

He cooled my fevered brow with a tender tongue, as his forebears licked the sores of the beggar Lazarus. Dogs are such cheering enthusiasts at everything they set their paw to. How would the Darling family have managed without nursemaid Nana? How sensible of Macbeth to throw them his physic.

They are nature's psychologists – 'Never trust a man who is not sound with dogs,' advised P. G. Wodehouse. They were sex educators centuries before Masters and Johnson. 'My daughter's getting married next month, doctor, and she doesn't know what she ought,' a Yorkshirewoman was quoted in *World Medicine*. 'I were waiting for the dog to come on heat so I could explain, but the dog died.'

Thackeray wagged his splendidly feathered tail. Dogs hailed as healers is a public relations exploit matching the donations of rapacious and polluting industry to medical foundations.

Last year, Manchester's Professor of Community Medicine took the lead on dogs. Our 6 million best friends annually bite 210,000 and infect 60,000 of their lovers. They cause 40 million quids' worth of road accidents, and pay towards it only $37\frac{1}{2}$p each.

Every day they leak a million gallons of urine and deposit 1,000 tons of poo-poos on the pavements. This is heavily loaded with the roundworm *Toxocara canis*, causing nasty things from itchy skin to blindness.

Already I could face the shame of appearance in court for not whisking Thackeray into the gutter, as he squats as swiftly and unexpectedly as a trout rising to the fly. Soon I may be legally forced to clear up after him, though I intend to avoid the reversal of nursing roles with Pampers.

Manchester has cured the dog-bite. Those not kept as stud-dogs would be castrated, making every breed as gentle as spaniels.

My agued hand fondled my medical attendant's dewlaps.

'Never, Thackeray, never!' I mumbled dry-mouthed. 'I vow they will have mine before yours.'

He barked joyfully.

Even Manchester agrees that dogs give tender companionship to humans living alone. It complains only that so many take their responsibilities towards their dog as lightly as towards their marriage – clearly unacceptable in any civilised community.

Thackeray and I passed the pyrexial hours together. I grew delirious. I believed him a consultant from the local hospital, who had the same expression of lugubrious preoccupation and quivering nose, caused by trying to be agreeable towards the patient while wondering what the devil was the matter with him.

He climbed on the bed. I let sleeping dogs lie. My family arrived home, thrust dog and patient into the cold and vigorously sprayed both of us and the bedclothes for fleas.

In the morning I was better, but poor Thackeray had to call the vet for canine flu.

I felt a terrible dirty dog.

August 1985

KEVIN
WOODCOCK

Profiteer's Lady. 'I SHALL CERTAINLY SEND FIDO TO A SHOW NEXT YEAR. NOT OF COURSE THAT HE WOULD WIN ANYTHING, BUT I WOULD LIKE HIM TO MEET SOME REALLY NICE DOGS.'

G. W. Stonier

CHARLES THE SECOND

There he comes, so bright, so elegant, stepping so lightly, as though the whole day were his. And so almost it is. Fashion, breeding, good looks and good manners, all seem in him combined. Who could withhold admiration? While he breathes the air, and treads the afternoon gravel, dandyism, you feel, still lives.

Whereby, as they say, hangs a tale.

Less than a year ago my friend X, who does not do too badly as a thriller writer, and whom you could count on for an hour's cheer at the local, was the most slovenly man alive. Tangled hair, horn-rims askew, most of his time spent in an old sports coat with an old pipe. Lodgings over an antique shop. Worked from eight to eleven in the morning, doing his three hundred words a day – never a word less or more – and leaving the day (as most of us see it) free. An enviable existence. Tens of thousands enjoyed his thrillers, though X himself, employing a pseudonym, was curiously ashamed of them.

His landlady patched his socks, cooked him nourishing stews, ran after him with a hat when it rained. He belonged to our Gibbons Society, which went about giving recitals, and was a fair if nervy tenor.

We first began to notice his absence when he failed to turn up for 'O clap your hands.' It didn't much matter, though being short he made a good middle man, but when the following night, at the repetition, there was still no sign of X and no word from him, questions began to be asked.

Was he ill, or away? Busy? It seemed unlikely, since the pub hadn't seen him either. Why hadn't he let us know?

Someone proposed dropping him a card, and there the matter rested.

Not for long, however. Next day there was news. X had a dog.

Oh, was that all!

A dog would suit X, who had never looked like settling down; and if he couldn't exactly bring him along, surely – with the landlady's help – there would be evenings off.

'You wait till you see him,' remarked our informant.

I happened to catch a sight of X that same afternoon. He appeared, I thought, much as usual, if a bit haggard and as though fiercely distracted; then I noticed the lead in his hand and, among shoppers passing and re-passing——

Good heavens! Such a barbered and clipped, smart, smiling, milk-chocolate-coloured poodle, standing three feet high, as you can't imagine! X's dog? It was unbelievable.

I began to cross, but the poodle had set off at a trot, in the most graceful way, and by the time the traffic had cleared they had vanished.

However, I picked up from others what had happened: X had obliged a friend by looking after the dog for a few days, the friend had taken a post abroad, and X had been persuaded to keep the dog on. He wasn't difficult to persuade.

But of all dogs a poodle! And of all poodles Charles! For I must admit I've never met anything quite so dignified or well bred in my life.

He was so quiet in the room that you might hardly have noticed him, but for a presence that imposed itself. If, somewhere at your back, he stretched or sighed – and this is an age for sighing, goodness knows – you'd forget it was Charles and wonder who it could be you were crowding from the fire. Happening to turn round at such a moment and meeting Charles' refined gaze, I was startled out of my composure. I laughed. He looked, with his fine, serious eyes and his floppy moustache, so exactly like Gorky, whose autobiography I had just been reading.

'He's like Gorky,' I said to X. X replied stiffly that Gorky was altogether shaggier, which was quite true; for on top of his head Charles sported not the wild growth of revolutionary sympathy but a frizz any actress of the Comédie Française might have borrowed.

X told me how sensitive and considerate Charles was, so that it was a shame even to let him think you might be laughing.

I did my best to make it up to Charles. I greeted him courteously. I looked up Gorky: there was really no resemblance. I brought him cracknels, and I never patted, I laid my hand on his shoulder as one might with an old friend.

As I might have done with X himself, but that now he was a quite different man, and changing day by day. He was growing exquisite to match Charles. Gone the disordered hair, the speckly bags, the mild grin, the whole easy existence we had envied; he now wore a suit of smart cut, his socks not only paired but sparkled, his shirt cuffs projected the three-quarters of an inch they should, and he might have been the author not of *Taradiddle, V.C.* but of *Zuleika Dobson.*

He explained, in a hesitating way, that one had certain responsibilities, duties to society, which he might have neglected. The public eye must be fed. There was Style. Quick ones and madrigals were a thing of the past.

After that I saw very little of X except in the distance. When I met him and Charles, I always bowed, and mastered an inclination – when we had passed – to stand and look back.

A fur-collared coat came into the picture. And taxis.

Charles started the taxi habit. Having one day grown tired after his walk round the park, he had presented himself at a taxi-rank with such authority that, unobtrusively reading the address on his collar, the man had opened the door and driven him home.

He got to know all the taxi-men and would hail a cab whenever he was in a hurry or felt slack.

Sometimes X was with him. Or one would be seen urging his driver on, in pursuit of the other. Soon it was taxis here, taxis everywhere.

X has moved from the antique shop, and now occupies a flat with a commanding view over the Park and two bathrooms – one presumably for Charles.

But he seems to lack the serenity that should go with position. Is this new life of ease beginning to tell? Are the bills mounting? The books not selling? Has Style invaded the sacred three hundred? I don't know.

Ah, here *he* comes – Charles, of course. How splendid he looks, how proud without disdain, beautiful without foppishness! But who leads the dog's life now? Not Charles the Second, as he rounds the corner, stepping on air.

For I have known Charles the First too; but that's another, and a much sadder, story.

'*Bye, dear – I'm just taking the hologram for a walk.*'

February 1955

'Play Mrs Barker that thing that made Rex bite Mrs Simpson.'

'Hat off in the House!'

McMurtry

THE PET SET

'How much is that doggy in the window? The
one with the waggly tail.'

'Excuse me, madam. I don't believe you've
paid for those tortoises.'

'I'm sorry, sir – we don't do part exchange.'

9

SCATTERED SHOWERS

'Soon be autumn – the rain's getting colder.'

Melvyn Bragg

RAINDROPS KEEP FALLING

You may think that a torrential August in Cumbria – when the country might just as well have been a boat out at sea, Keswick topping the rain-charts every day – would be, well, a wash-out. Not unlike Dorothy Wordsworth's experiences in her *Journals*: 'Went for a walk – soaked: came back to poddish and rum.' 'Went for the post – soaked – came back and resolved to live in Provence.' The fells were under cloud, the lakes all but joined up, rivers burst their banks, outside our cottage the track became a substantial mountain stream; the roof leaked, the anoraks had to be renewed; but the water-falls were astounding.

That was my one half-good idea this August. To the waterfalls! Usually, they dash and tumble; a little plashing here, a show of spurting spuming there; a swift side-step around a rock: an unexciting sight. I had always thought that those who wrote of the district in the late eighteenth century – and those who painted it – exaggerated the 'terror', the 'horror', the dreaded grandeur of it all. Partly, it was the fashion: by such hyperbole you proved your sensibility; partly, it was because it was good old hack 'em along journalism; and partly, I now know, especially with regard to the water-falls, it was because they must have had weather like we have had this August.

We went to the waterfalls and came away, drenched as trout. The Cataract of Lodore is possibly the most painted, and thanks to Southey's poem, the best known waterfall:

How does the water

Come down the Lodore?
My little boy asked me
Thus, once on a time;
His description of it, over scores of lines, had never matched my own experience:
Rising and leaping
Sinking and creeping
Swelling and sweeping
Showering and spraying.
Or,
And whizzing and hissing,
And dripping and skipping
And hitting and splitting
And shining and turning.
Still less,
And bubbling and trembling
And grumbling and rumbling and tumbling
And clattering and battering and shattering.
And not at all,
And rushing and flushing and brushing and gushing
And flapping and rapping and clapping and slapping.
And so on: I need quote no more – you probably have it by heart.

Well, it was even better than that.

I have to admit that we drove there. I had wanted to walk but the children had already been skin-saturated twice that day; I then suggested we row up the lake from Friar's Crag to the Lodore landing-stage, but there were no volunteers for bailing duty. The car had it. By the time we had walked across the road, up the path – money in the honesty box – and into the wood which rears sheer up the Borrowdale volcanic road, we were sodden.

The cataract made up for everything. The water, though mainly white, was brown-tinged, and it seemed to hurl itself out of the mountain in what, at the first impression, felt like a solid mass; more like a rush of rock than a fall of water. We went to the foot of it by the stream and looked up into a fuming gorge of force which would have cowed and impressed to 'terror' anyone – Romantic, realist or sceptic – because what it made you was fearful. As we started to climb up the side of the fall, the slippery rocks meant that the others decided to go back. And yes, I went on alone.

It was tremendous, Southey was right, Constable was right, Farrington was right, Gray was right – what power it had. About a third of the way up I, foolishly, went out into the middle of it, where there was a bare rock, and looked directly into the eye of this pounding of water. The roar of it sounded as if the volcanic mountain had opened its jaws; the fury of the pelting water was frightening; the rock was very cold. You could understand, though, how minds as extraordinary as that of Coleridge could have delighted in the extreme sensations brought on by the wildness of the display. Water, dark rocks, overhanging trees, a mountain staring up like some ancient beast ready to pound down its hooves on you, and above that a turbulence of clouds which – I swear – then collided into thunder and flashed out lightning.

My rock was like Grace Darling's rowing-

THE PIC-NIC.

Contented Man (loq.) 'WHAT A NICE DAMP PLACE WE'VE SECURED; AND HOW VERY FORTUNATE WE ARE IN THE WEATHER! IT WOULD HAVE BEEN SO PROVOKING FOR US ALL TO HAVE BROUGHT OUR UMBRELLAS, AND THEN TO HAVE HAD A FINE DAY!! GLASS OF WINE, BRIGGS, EH?'

boat as the melodrama hissed and volleyed and flashed about. A great deal of the poetry was based on an apprehension heightened by such dramatic fear. I slithered back across the side of the fall and considered climbing to the top in this Gothic scenario. I voted against it. The bolts of lightning which seemed to be pitched very accurately at the top of the falls were probably the deciding factor in the final ballot.

Everywhere we went after that, we saw the old waterfalls gorged on the rain and the great vats of water which must have collected in the hills – and new waterfalls hurtling to join in the fun down little tracks in the fellside which had been dry for years.

Occasionally we did other things. We went on one of those lovely Edwardian boats around Derwent Water and I stood out at the front, mummified in anorak and overtrousers, feeling like a hero in Conrad outfacing a hurricane in the China Seas. Once again we were bidden to the oldest sports event in the north-west, Grasmere, by Sir

John Burgess, to record and enjoy the allday wrestling, the fell running, the company, the picnic and the wine served in plastic cups – but even here, though the rain almost held off, we were not convinced, and lookouts were posted to keep an eye out for the rain – which crashed down again at the end of the day, through the night, in the morning. We attempted to pursue a balance by ensuring that the inside was as thoroughly watered as the outside; we built log fires and made daring raids on the crazy-putting green; we walked through the woods and discovered the limitations of trees as shelter; we chalked up the waterfalls.

One day, towards the end of the month, the sun came up, the clouds went away. It was hot, not merely warm, and there was no wind. We stayed at home and looked at it suspiciously, even resentfully, spoiling all our plans. I watched the cricket.

September 1985

Graham

HEAT-WAVE

'It's cooling a little now, thank goodness!'

Ann Leslie
IN THE HEAT OF THE DAY

Here comes summer! Rise up my love, my fair one, and come away, for lo, the winter is past, the rain is over and gone, and by the dried-up waters of Babylon the Water Board doth sit down and weep. The time of trannies in the park is come, the ant is in the salad-cream, the barbecue is cleansed of mouse-droppings – so gather thou up the chap-stick, the calomine, the Enterovioform, the bug-repellent, and let us together seek The Sun . . .

Not, of course, English sun – pleasant inoffensive yellow stuff as bland as English custard. To that sun, their own sun, the tribes of urban Britain respond with quaint folk ritual: now is the time of the tying of knots in hankies, and of placing them upon heads; of the rolling up of the trouser-leg, of the offering up of pale gnarled knees like bindweed roots to the air; of the ritual scattering of lolly-sticks upon the municipal greenswards, and of the uttering of gloomy incantations:'phew-what-a-scorcher','can't-last-mark-my-words-can't-last' . . .

This gentle, eccentric sun is not the stuff that exotic dreams are made on. No, sexy sun, the sun of Bacchus and of Pan, the sun which burns off clothes, inhibitions and skin, is *foreign* sun.

Into its alchemical cauldron the northern tribes pour the base-metal of their everyday selves, and dream that somehow, this time, they will become transmuted into creatures of drossless, glorious gold, inwardly marked by that sacred fire forever . . .

To you, I am Mr Thickpenny of Sales, but behold I have been to Toledo (Optional Coach Trip and Packed Lunch for Bullfight Extra) and I have smelt the dark perfume of blood in the sand, and drunk deep of death in the afternoon and lo, I am El Thickpenny and beneath my Raelbrook-toplin my soul doth wear the suit of lights and . . . ('yes dear, the usual – iced bun and only one sugar please') . . .

In these liberating pagan fires, the loins of suburban dentists stir with new, unfettered lusts, and mild accountants remember Gauguin and on their dream horizon glimpse steaming black *wahines* with fat toes and sumptuous breasts, walloping joyously through Freudian sea-spray, with garlands of hibiscus dripping from their thick, hot chocolaty thighs. Oh how gorgeous are these fantasies, what food for the psyche and the self-esteem . . .

To you, I am Mr Fosdyke, your nosey neighbourhood VAT-man, but behold I have been to Serengeti (Air-Conditioned Safari Landrover and don't approach the lions please) and lo, I am Fosdyke of the River, Fosdyke the White Hunter, Rider Fosdyke, with the amulet of elephant's hair about my bronzed wrist. And come eventide at No. 9, Bannerman Villas, you will see me scan the lupin beds for spoor of snail and hunt the earwig herds across the back-yard veldt and . . . ('no, sir, I'm afraid bay-trees aren't zero-rated unless you intend to eat them') . . .

What gives Foreign Sun its magic properties is simply its rarity value: most people only get to experience it for a fortnight or so each year – they don't have to live with it long enough for its fantasy-inducing ingredient to wear off. If, however, like me, you were actually brought up in Foreign Sun (in my case the Indian variety), you tend to regard it with a more jaundiced air.

Day after day, year after year, I watched the beastly stuff banging down out of the sky until the earth shimmered and rang like a vast brass gong. When it all became unbearable, the memsahibs of the Raj took out their Horrocks frocks and white cardies and gardening trugs and, in a cloud of mothballs and

→ 177

Bill Tidy

FROZEN NORTH

WE WERE SO POOR WE USED TO COME UP HERE FOR US HOLIDAYS

*'Well, if outside lav's frozen, you'll just have
to use inside lav won't you.'*

'Nay, Arnold ... not every one frozen?'

'How many times ... you don't wear a flat hat for t'match in this weather!'

'Doctor, CPL's managing director says does the cause of death have to be starvation?'

'Try and hold on, luv – Dr McKechnie and the Lower Milnthorpe clog dancers are nearly through!'

small children, headed for the hill-station, a corner of that foreign field which was forever Esher.

And so my youthful fantasies were never of the sun: to me, Eros dwelt in a distant West-of-Suez world of dampness and moss and dripping chestnut trees and Bath Olivers and the Army and Navy Stores. My dream lover was not rippling his pectorals on some desert steed, nor riding the wine-dark sea, naked, upon a caique. He was sitting, Burberry-clad, in a red London bus amidst steaming rubber macs and wet socks; our lips would one day meet – not to the dreary sound of the cicada – but to the erotic hissing of gas-lamps on some mournful, windswept railway station; our bodies would one day merge – not in some horrid gnat-filled tropic grove – but in a dark and woolly room smelling of firelighters and lino and generations of old, damp dogs.

Of course, like all fantasies, this 'oh-for-a-beaker-of-the-wet-North' version wore pretty thin as soon as I'd had to sample its reality for a few weeks; but hey-ho, that's the way the fantasy-cookie crumbles.

Fantasies are only fun when they remain fantasies: their magic must never be soiled with attempts at realisation. This is particularly true of the 'back-to-the-simple-life-of-the-soil' dream which tends to smite the town-dweller while his mind is befuddled by summer sun.

He gets into his Cortina, finds a field full of buttercups and in no time at all he's skipping about trilling 'hello birds! hello sky! and where's the nearest estate-agent?' Even I, urban to the core, and liable to get fidgety when deprived of the sight of tarmac for too long, have felt dangerously tempted by this particular loony dream.

Luckily, I realise that what I really want is 'pretend' country, art-director's country, the telly-country of Kelloggs and Vitbe and Bulmer's. A country of mists and mellow fruitfulness, and cosy cottagers with cosy cottages, slopped overall with art-director's thatch and art-director's roses; a mythic Kodachrome land which neither moth nor rust nor beetle can corrupt.

Real country makes me nervous: real country always seems so full of mud, feathers and death. You go there for peace and quiet, and the welkin rings with the scream of the killer and the killed: owls murdering mice, foxes mugging chickens, gangs of rooks savaging worms, poachers shooting pheasants, game-keepers shooting poachers – it's all a fearful strain on delicate city nerves.

Real farms, as opposed to the things you see on Dairylea wrappings, are stinking, ramshackle dung-heaps full of rural Peckinpahs going about their ceaseless round of branding, slaughtering, strangling and castrating. Real country folk are perfectly frightful about animals: to me, that's a pretty flopsy-wopsy bunny-rabbit exquisitely ornamenting the gentle wold; to them, it's just stew-on-legs, incomplete without buckshot and oven. To me, those gambolling lambs are symbols of innocence and joy; to them, they're just woolly cutlets awaiting their appointment with slicer and mint sauce.

All this rural savagery seething and ravening about the hedgerows is thoroughly brutalising to civilised city folk. Better by far that we seek our dreams in foreign climes where we cannot linger, and dreams do not have time to die . . .

To you, I am nice Miss Simpkins of the Borough Library, but beneath this angora woolly, my breasts glow with wild Aegean fire, and ('I'm sorry, Mrs Kenworthy, but "Jaws" is still out, and your husband's overdue on "Confessions of a Meter-Reader"') and I have seen the eyes of waiters grow heavy with desire across the inky octopus, and lo, I am Helen, and behind these specs mine eyes have seen the broken wall, the burning tower, and Agamemnon dead . . .

June 1976

Jonathan Sale

ILL MET BY SUNLIGHT

There was this lecturer speaking on the end of the world, which will happen in five thousand million years, when the sun becomes vaster and vaster until its swirling volume actually balloons out to engulf the innermost planets, scorching the rest with its unbelievable . . .

At this point in the lecture, a man in the front row begins screaming and foaming at the mouth, babbling about 'Death and destruction! Death and destruction!'

'It's all right,' says the lecturer, patting him on the cheek, 'it's not for another five thousand million years.'

'Thank God for that,' says the man, sitting up and straightening his tie, 'I thought you said *four* thousand million years.'

THE BRITISH CHARACTER
KEEN INTEREST IN THE WEATHER

Well, scientists late last night were commenting that according to their observations it's a very old joke, but my own calculations show that it's a very old solar system, so there. But it makes you wonder as you work out the final details of a summer holiday under the sky, exactly what is happening to the sun and the weather over the next few decades. Will there be enough of both to go around?

'Astronomical theories suggest that the sun has been effectively constant in radiation over the last few 100,000 million years. Of course, the sun will eventually swell up until it swallows the innermost planets, but not for another f . . .'

'Four thousand million years?' I asked the man holding the interplanetary fort at the *New Scientist,* feeling a bit of a turn coming on.

'Five thousand million years,' he reassured me. 'There is,' he added, 'speculation that little fluctuations may cause Ice Ages. It's a very open question.'

To close the question, scientists are drilling holes in the Arctic's ice to see what the weather was doing all those millennia ago when the bottom bits first dropped below freezing. They are examining the growth of lichen at the foot of glaciers to see how many fractions of an inch per hundred years they are coming or going. They are poking about in the innards of elderly trunks, amid cries of 'Meteorologist, spare that tree!' to see from the rings when it was a bit parky over the last few hundred years and when it was rather on the warm side. They are finding that sunspots, those massive storms on the sun's surface, may be able to help them with their enquiries. They are wondering if the way the continents drift around the surface of the world is the cause of differing climates. They are also, for all I know, taking electron microscopes to bits of seaweed on the window-ledges, feeding their rheumatic pains into computers, and holding conferences to discuss the proposition that 'If it rains on St Médard's Day (June 8), it will rain for six weeks after, unless St Barnabas (June 11) has put everything right,' which is not only an ancient proverb but a Swiss ancient proverb, precision built to incredible accuracy by the country which gave us the cuckoo-clock. And some of them are of the very firm opinion that they have no opinion about a forthcoming Ice Age or hundred years of sizzling to come.

'We can't, because nobody knows,' said the man at the Met. Office in London when I asked him to make a stab at the next thirty years of weather. 'We don't like to do forecasts more than a few days ahead. There *are* theories about climatic trends, but the Met. Office is not a party to them. Why don't you try our head office at Bracknell?' And off he went to take the temperature on the Air Ministry roof; well, that's my theory.

'Looking ahead?' exclaimed Mr Kevin Miles, a Principal Scientific Officer at Bracknell, working in the field of climatic change. 'You should have gone to that man in the television programme who stands on Brighton pier and looks ahead from there. We're more cautious.'

'Well, is it getting colder?'

'I should be against that. The balance from the indications from the various theories is that this is unlikely. Let's take the various things that are said to affect the global mean temperature.' We took the increase in the carbon dioxide content of the earth, which, I gather, some rash fellows think might actually warm the place up by half a degree Centigrade by the end of the century. But bear in mind that: 'From about 1885 to 1940 the Northern Hemisphere rose by about 0.6 degrees Centigrade, which is a pretty big increase; and carbon dioxide probably was responsible for about a quarter of that. From 1940 to the end of the sixties, there was a fall of about 0.3 degrees; volcanic dust may have been responsible for some of that. I would like to say 0.2 or 0.3 degrees of the cooling and warming is *not* explained by these two factors.' So what can it be, this mysterious Ingredient X in the weather game – bad vibrations in Bradford affecting the Gulf Stream? Are scientists working on a theory that Alien Beings from Alpha Centauri are causing droughts in allotments in Sussex and floods in parts of Devon?

'I should be rather inclined to say that the 0.2 up and down represents natural fluctuations that the climate is capable of, a shuffling round of the heat, if you like, between oceans and clouds and so on. Is further cooling going to go on in the next few decades? We put dust up into the atmos-phere as a result of our activities, but a lot of factors tell against that being influential. If you try to make measurements of the turbidity of the atmosphere, they don't in every way show an increase in turbidity. There are no measurements that show conclusively that the sun's output has altered this century; it's not proved conclusively that sunspots mean more or less heat reaching the outer atmosphere.' Mr Miles, as you gather, sticks to caution in forecasting.

So with that cautionary note from the most academic of experts, we'll just move over to the weather outlook from some of the more frightening of meteorologists. We can expect a very heavy fall of Dr Terence Meaden

'It's the gardener, dear – I've no objection to him getting a bit mellow, but I'm a little concerned about his fruitfulness.'

whose *Journal of Meteorology,* edited from his home in Trowbridge, Wilts, discusses not only the Colder Britain Theory but the outbreak of tornadoes. These have apparently been increasing, with the 1976 score at 34, which is way above Oklahoma, tornado capital of the USA, and Dr Meaden fears that they are getting more frequent and stronger, and has founded the Tornado and Storm Research Organisation to prove it.

However, the mainstream of doomwatchers see the falling thermometer as the big threat, leading possibly to a return to the age when England was a frozen desert surrounded by mile-thick sheets of ice and glaciers ruled the roost of even such sunspots as California and Mexico. 'The great thaw came only ten thousand years ago,' writes Nigel Calder in his comprehensible – even to me – survey of theories, *The Weather Machine* (BBC Publications, £3.25). 'Now very recent discoveries imply that the chance of the next ice age starting in our own lifetimes is not zero.'

Readers will please forgive the hysterical outburst there; 'not zero' is the meteorological equivalent of running naked down the M1 yelling, 'Run for your lives – the glaciers have reached Watford!' But then he has been talking to scientists who have noticed that there is more ice getting in the way of shipping around Greenland than ever in living memory. He has talked to Danish scientists who have gazed into Arctic ice and, projecting the fluctuations of the sun hidden therein, suggested a cooling until the 1980s, a slight warming until about 2015, and then several centuries banging our hands together to keep the circulation going. Moreover, those who make it their business to study the rate of growth of trees in Lapland conclude that we have at least 100 years of worsened climate to look forward to, if past cycles mean anything. Glaciers in that part of the world have been melting during the century – but not so much of late. Others swear that manmade dust – mentioned by the Met. Office – is in fact responsible for the present cooling and also drying up of parts of the globe. Their rivals hold to the story that the ice sheets of the Antarctic are slipping, possibly to result in tidal waves and an Ice Age in the North, bringing sea-levels everywhere 180 feet higher.

My own theory is that I agree with all who say that the weather is a vastly complicated machine that needs a lot more work by the eminent and skilled men already engaged on it, and that, as one writing this at what I fear can't be more than 30 feet above sea level, it's about time we had a lifeboat on the premises. I would adduce one piece of evidence for your consideration, taken from an authority in which I have read as widely as any man alive, the 'Weather' section of *Cassell's Classified Quotations,* 1921: 'As the Devil said to Noah, "It's bound to clear up!" (Proverbial saying).'

June 1976